Praise for *Preaching the Go...*

In a day when many wonder if preaching is little more than a solo performance of self meant to build a platform of personal followers, Dr. Jennifer Ackerman offers us a call, instruction, and demonstration of preaching at its most communal, transformative, collaborative, embodied, and proclamatory. It breathes the gospel. It exudes good news. It teaches skills and gives instructions that are often neglected. Best of all, it practices what it "preaches." In Psalm 85, truth, love, justice, and peace all come together in one lyrical affirmation. This book gives us a glimpse of what that kind of preaching could be, and hope that we preachers can learn to offer it. It is a celebration of what a community of proclamation and demonstration can *form* in both preachers and their congregants.

—Rev. Dr. Tod Bolsinger, executive director, Church
Leadership Institute, and author of *Tempered Resilience:
How Leaders Are Formed in the Crucible of Change*

From her lived experience as practitioner and professor, Ackerman provides a timely call to proclaim the gospel of God made known in Jesus Christ. Translating it for the twenty-first century as "justice," Ackerman recovers the biblical testimony to the inbreaking of the kingdom of God. *Preaching the Gospel of Justice* gleans from Ackerman's real-life pastoral experiences, offering much-needed good news in a culture in trauma. Reminding preachers that their task requires intentionality, inquiry, and innovation that hold fast to the biblical witness to God's promises, this book exemplifies how sermons need to be practical, prophetic, and provocative.

—Rev. Dr. Joy J. Moore, visiting professor of religion
and Chapman-Benson Lecturer, Huntingdon College;
professor of biblical preaching, Luther Seminary

Jennifer Ackerman writes as a practitioner: not in an ivory tower, but from pulpits, streets, and around coffee tables. She is a prophetic preacher who, through the Micah Group, has engaged preachers across diverse social and ethnic backgrounds living with the questions in this book: How can we preach the whole good news of God's justice without getting fired or burned out in a society that has whittled the gospel into a self-help meme? I'm a more grounded preacher for having met Jennifer and the preacher friends she introduced me to through the Micah Group. In this book, you are welcoming a preacher, a leader, and a friend who will accompany you on your journey of prophetic faithfulness.

—Rev. Samuel Son, manager of diversity and reconciliation, Presbyterian Mission Agency

In this brief, accessible, and multilayered resource, Jennifer Ackerman offers an inviting menu of food for thought for preachers: solid homiletics, ideas for spiritual practices, and provocative glimpses into the preaching art from varied and insightful voices. I came away refreshed and inspired to examine and reinvigorate my approach to sharing the good news.

—Rev. Wendy S. Tajima, executive presbyter, Presbytery of San Gabriel, Presbyterian Church (USA)

Whether you are new to pulpit ministry or have a well-worn path to the pulpit from throughout your ministry life, Dr. Ackerman has given the church a timely gift with this fresh and insightful text. She writes from her embodied ministerial life, as well as reaching across the width of the body of Christ to the margins to rediscover a vision for a preaching ministry centered on the gospel of justice. She gives a compelling vision of the art of homiletics coupled with some practical considerations in preparing a sermon (praxis). She rightfully includes sermons as illustrations for her vision. I highly recommend this book!

—Rev. Dr. Bret M. Widman, director of Contextual and Lifelong Learning and associate professor of ministry, North Park Theological Seminary

PREACHING THE GOSPEL OF JUSTICE

PREACHING THE GOSPEL OF JUSTICE

Good News in Community

JENNIFER L. ACKERMAN

Fortress Press
Minneapolis

PREACHING THE GOSPEL OF JUSTICE
Good News in Community

Library of Congress Cataloging-in-Publication Data

Names: Ackerman, Jennifer, author.
Title: Preaching the Gospel of justice : good news in community / Jennifer
  Lynn Ackerman.
Description: Minneapolis : Fortress Press, [2024]
Identifiers: LCCN 2023041731 (print) | LCCN 2023041732 (ebook) | ISBN
  9781506495668 (print) | ISBN 9781506495675 (ebook)
Subjects: LCSH: Justice--Religious aspects--Christianity. |
  Justice--Biblical teaching. | Christianity and justice.
Classification: LCC BS680.J8 A254 2024 (print) | LCC BS680.J8 (ebook) |
  DDC 251--dc23/eng/20231214
LC record available at https://lccn.loc.gov/2023041731
LC ebook record available at https://lccn.loc.gov/2023041732

Cover design: Kristin Miller (series design by Emily Harris)

Print ISBN: 978-1-5064-9566-8
eBook ISBN: 978-1-5064-9567-5

CONTENTS

ACKNOWLEDGMENTS

This book is largely a product of my work with the Micah Groups community of church leaders committed to the convergence of worship, preaching, and justice, and especially the wisdom and partnership of Micah Mobilizers Joy Johnson, Jin Cho, Bret Widman, and Mary Ellen Azada. It is also a product of all that I learn, year after year, from eager and earnest preaching students in search of their voices of proclamation.

Thank you to Inés Velásquez-McBryde, Brenda Bertrand, Cindy S. Lee, and Mark Labberton for trusting me with their seasoned and prophetic voices. Thank you to Carey Newman, the first to suggest my voice as an author should be heard, and to my editor, Laura Gifford, the first to suggest this book should be written. Thank you to countless friends and colleagues who have been encouragers and conversation partners, especially Keith Bundy for the Lent writing that got me started; Rachel Paprocki, who found a method in my madness; and Jenn Graffius, whose kick in the pants pushed me over the finish line.

Lastly, my orientation toward a life of worship and community is surely thanks to my parents, Marsha and Eric Ackerman, who organized our family's rhythms around the rhythms of worship. Dad, you were the first preacher I ever heard, and a voice I continue to hear today.

Introduction

One of the questions I'm often asked about my work as a professor of preaching is something along the lines of, "What is the biggest mistake you see students make in their preaching?" I don't really accept the premise of the question, in terms of "mistakes," since preaching is a lifelong journey with all manner of pitfalls to encounter along the way, and we should all be so fortunate as to have opportunity to learn from those pitfalls no matter the point in our journey. Quibbles over semantics aside, however, the prevailing issue I find myself pointing out in student sermons is that they often fail to include Good News, instead focusing almost exclusively on how we are to behave as people of God and disciples of Christ. This is certainly one very important part of the equation, but what hope do we have of successfully conforming to the will of God if we do not first understand how God's grace and mercy and love have equipped us to do so?

In addition to teaching preaching, I also direct an institute for preachers who are committed to the convergence of worship, preaching, and justice. From this vantage point, I am often asked questions like, "How can I do a better job preaching justice?" or "How can I convince my church they should care about justice?" My answer here is the same: preach Good News!

As far as I'm concerned, there is no distinction between the gospel's message of grace and its message of justice—they are one and the same. If we are living in the freedom afforded to us by the love and forgiveness of God, made possible by the saving work of Christ and continually empowered by the presence of the Holy Spirit, then our only adequate response is to seek justice, love mercy, and walk humbly with God. In other words, if we are truly following Jesus, then we are earnestly seeking to love God *and neighbor*, which means we are seeking to do justice.

The task of every preacher and of every sermon is to preach the gospel of justice. There are not some Sundays for justice sermons and other Sundays for evangelism sermons or stewardship sermons or Advent sermons or Lent sermons. All sermons that proclaim the Good News of God's inbreaking presence through Christ and the overall witness of scripture are sermons of justice. Some preaching traditions have long understood this to be true—in Black Church traditions, for example, and others rooted in a liberation theology perspective. The preachers I know from these contexts don't call what they do *justice preaching*; it's just *preaching*.

We happen to be living in a time when public debate over social justice issues has become the norm. What was once considered impolite to discuss in polite company—that is, in privileged company—is now a kind of litmus test between the antiquated conservative and the reckless progressive. The reality is, both sides distort the gospel of justice by claiming it as their own.

Preaching the gospel of justice is not about using the pulpit to dictate legislative agendas or policy reform, but to focus our attention on the exceedingly abundant power of God at work in us (Ephesians 3). Sometimes this will, in fact, lead to social action and calls for dismantling unjust systems, but mostly it will tune our ears to listen for the Spirit's whispers toward seeking justice in all moments of life—the extraordinary and the mundane.

This kind of preaching, then, is a matter of routine, not a special occasion. In observing preachers who have adopted such a preaching routine, I've come to appreciate that it involves a few key commitments:

- **A Call to Community:** The transformative gift of the gospel certainly has personal implications for each individual, but the full extent of Kingdom work can only be fully embraced as a practice of community. Preaching the gospel of justice means much more than one person speaking and gathered individuals listening—it is an ongoing dialogue that informs, nurtures, and evaluates a commitment to practices of justice throughout communities of faith.
- **A Covenant of Justice:** Preachers must avoid the tendency to make justice sermons primarily a personal to-do list. Ultimately, justice is in God's hands, and we are mere agents. Our work of justice can only ever be in response to the good gifts we've received from God, and that is the Good News begging to be proclaimed. Preaching the gospel of justice means going deep into scripture, not wide into proof texting, so we might see more clearly the covenantal love God extends to us and in which God calls us to participate.
- **A Prophetic Witness:** Justice-leaning churches today have become very adept at participating in social justice causes through community organizing,

protest marches, and networking with both sacred and secular non-profit organizations. Engaging in such tangible action is a vital part of our work, but the church is called to do something more than our secular co-laborers—we must be the prophetic voice in the wilderness that reminds the world that our hope is in the power and purposes of God, not in our own best intentions. Preaching the gospel of justice means inviting the disruption of God's truth to help us see a different path forward and learn to march according to the rhythm of the Kingdom of God rather than the rhythm of the empire.

Finally, preaching the gospel of justice is simply not possible outside an ongoing commitment to drawing near to the heart of God in worship. Thus, the commitments above ultimately culminate in **A Life of Worship.**

When the Body of Christ gathers to worship, we exercise our call to community, remember the bonds of God's covenant of justice with us, and begin to embody the prophetic witness of disciples on a Kingdom journey. Our liturgical acts of praise, confession, meditating on the Word, or engaging in prayer are all preparation and practice for living our calling as disciples of Jesus. As we grow more fully into this calling, our liturgical worship and the worship of our lives become more and more intertwined, and we are more and more equipped to embody the gospel of justice inside and outside the sanctuary.

As preachers, we are practical theologians. Our work is not merely theoretical, it is a work of practice. We practice our theology through lives of worship and proclamation of sermons, facilitating our communities' practices. It only makes sense to me, then, to engage any conversation about preaching as a discussion of both theory and praxis. As such, you will read plenty here about my theology and the theories behind my preaching methodology and pedagogy, but you will also find practical resources and ideas to engage some of those theories in your own work. (See, especially, *Appendix B: Praxis Resources*.) I've also tried to quite literally practice what I preach by beginning each chapter with a homiletical reflection on a scripture text that provides foundational biblical theology for the core commitments under discussion.

As a special gift, four extraordinary preachers from Fuller Theological Seminary have allowed me to dialogue with a sermon each of them preached at an All-Seminary Chapel service. These are exemplars of what I believe it means to preach a gospel of justice. Only excerpts of the sermons are included in my discourses with them, but a full transcript of each is included in *Appendix A*. I hope you will read each sermon and experience for yourself the prophetic witness each has offered. (Better yet, follow the provided links to hear an audio recording of each sermon or watch each chapel service video.)

I pray this book may be a resource to preachers who have been awakened, reawakened, or are just awakening to a call to preach the gospel of justice. May we all rest in the assurance that we are mere agents of the work God has already done, is doing, and will continue to do. The most remarkable part of the Good News is that we are not called to do justice by ourselves, nor could we ever hope to do so. Good News proclamation testifies to a true encounter with Christ, the Living Word, who knows we must be prodded, encouraged, comforted, and challenged as a community of discerners and disciples wrestling with the mysteries of our faith.

CHAPTER 1

A Call to Community

For this reason I bow my knees before the Father, from
whom every family in heaven and on earth takes
its name. I pray that, according to the riches of his
glory, he may grant that you may be strengthened
in your inner being with power through his Spirit
and that Christ may dwell in your hearts through
faith, as you are being rooted and grounded
in love. I pray that you may have the power to
comprehend, with all the saints, what is the breadth
and length and height and depth and to know the
love of Christ that surpasses knowledge, so that
you may be filled with all the fullness of God.

Now to him who by the power at work within us is able
to accomplish abundantly far more than all we can
ask or imagine, to him be glory in the church and in
Christ Jesus to all generations, forever and ever. Amen.

—Ephesians 3:14–21

In Paul's letter to the Church in Ephesus, he spends chapters one through three outlining what he believes to be God's plan for the redemption of the world through the crucified, exalted, cosmic Christ. Chapters four through six reveal how this plan will be enacted by people of faith called to be the Body of Christ. Before making the homiletical turn to part two, Paul pauses the theological tone painting for this extraordinarily pastoral moment at the end of chapter three. He is on his knees in prayer for the sake of the whole family of God—every family in heaven and on earth—invoking the power of the Holy Spirit to do a mighty work in *us*; for the power of Christ to dwell in *us*; for the boundless presence of Christ's love and wisdom to fill *us*. Paul's singular attention to this most plural communal calling rests, literally, at the center of his message for the Ephesians. The benedictory nature of verses 20–21 is not so much a sending out as a drawing in. God can and will and is doing exceedingly abundantly more than anything our myopic individual imaginations could conceive because of the power at work within *us*, as agents of Christ, who serve the inbreaking of God in our world for all generations, forever and ever.

Most of Paul's letters are considered "occasional letters"—written to a specific person or community for a specific occasion, which essentially means that we get to read someone else's mail. We are more than mere voyeurs, however, since these letters form a critical piece of the canon of Holy Scripture, meaning that we believe God intends this mail for all of us in today's church, just as much as Paul intended it for those early churches. I believe this is particularly true of the letter to the Ephesians, which does not address specific issues raised by a particular church (like 1 and 2 Corinthians, for example), but instead addresses fundamental theology for the shaping of the universal church of

Christ. In fact, many biblical scholars believe that this letter was not written specifically for the Church in Ephesus; instead, it was something more like a form letter: "Dear Church fill-in-the-blank."[1] In some ancient manuscripts, the salutation of verse one reads, "To God's holy people in Ephesus," while others are addressed to another church, and still others to no church at all.

All of this underscores the fact that Paul's uniformly plural language in this letter must be understood as applicable to the *us* of all generations from yesterday, today, and tomorrow. It must also be understood that we're not talking about you + you + me = us or the letter's author + reader = us. Rather, Ephesians is an entirely plural message about *us* as a worshiping community; *us* as the universal church; *us* as the Body of Christ.

The message of Ephesians must not be reduced to an individual, personal admonition that turns us inward toward a private reckoning of *my* heart and *my* mind and the extent to which Christ is dwelling in *me*. Attention to our own hearts is certainly one aspect of the call, but appropriate attention can only be given when we understand that "God chose *us* before the creation of the world" means God chose *us* as the church. God intended *we as a church* to be holy and blameless (1:4). *We as a church* are alive together with Christ, and thus by grace we have been saved (2:5). We aren't chosen to be individuals who have entirely private and separate relationships with Jesus, and who just happen to get together on Sundays to talk about it. We are chosen to be a collective community, living together in a different way, a way that points to Jesus. We are working together to live in God's grace and the redemption of Christ.

In the late 2000s, I served as the Director of Worship for First Presbyterian Church of Berkeley, CA. Twice each year, on New Members Sunday, all those feeling called to join our community knelt in front of the congregation as a pastor anointed them with oil, saying, "You are now a member of First Presbyterian Church of Berkeley, and so you belong to us, and we belong to you."

It was my job to organize this ritual. I made sure the kneelers were in place, that the pastor had the oil, and that everyone lined up in the right order. But for years, I never went through the ritual myself. I *worked* for the church; I didn't need to be a *member* of the church. That seemed like too much commitment.

Then one day I began to sense a call to enter the ordination process, which meant I would have to be an official member of the church, so I found myself adding my own name to the list of congregants to be received on the next New Member Sunday. When the day came, I walked up the aisle from my usual place at the soundboard in the back and knelt down in front of the congregation. As my eyes scanned the many faces of this community that I knew and loved so well, I felt Pastor Debbie's thumb making the sign of the cross in oil on my forehead, and I heard her say to me, "Now you belong to us and we belong to you."

I didn't think it would mean anything to me. After all, I'd been part of this community for years already, and this was just rubber stamping the deal. Yet something happened in that moment. It wasn't an empty ritual. I felt God's presence. I felt God's hand on me. I understood, in a different way, what it meant to belong to God; what it meant to belong to the Body of Christ; what it meant to be an *us*.

Today, some fifteen years later, my usual place in worship is no longer at the soundboard in the back, but the pulpit in the front. Sunday after Sunday I scan the many faces of assorted congregations at which I am most often a guest preacher, so they are not known to me in the same way, and yet I continue to feel that sense of communal belonging together as an *us*. At the close of each service, I raise my hands above the congregation and declare the benediction of Ephesians 3: *Now to God, who has done exceedingly abundantly more than all we can ask or even imagine, according to the power that is at work in us; to this God be all glory in the church and in Christ Jesus both now and forevermore.* Then I hold my hands outward, inviting all to be drawn into this message, declaring, "And all God's people said. . .," to which the gathered community resoundingly responds in unison, "Amen!"

When the invitation is before us, we can't help but be swept up in this vision of abundant life. God's vision for us is so much bigger than our own, but we get trapped in the shallowness of our own vision—a result of the burdens that we bear, or if you prefer, of the sin that we carry, and we are inevitably pushed toward smallness. God sees us in our shallow, burdened, sinful smallness, and says, "I want more for you. I want you to live abundantly, and I've given you everything you need to do that." We grow out of our smallness when we realize the *you* is plural.

Preaching Is Personal and Communal

The purpose of preaching is to proclaim the gospel—the Good News of God for the people of God; the amazing grace that enables us to flourish and thrive through the tedium and suffering, joy and celebration, doubt and confusion, gifts and challenges of life. This Good News is both extraordinarily personal and inescapably communal. True discipleship as followers of Jesus Christ will reveal that the seemingly private gift of redemption is actually a catalyst toward a more public, continuing transformation. As we inch closer and closer to having the same mind in us that is in Christ, we come to understand that true redemption is only realized through the power of humility, not through the power of strength (Philippians 2).

In proclaiming this Good News, the role of the preacher is, likewise, extraordinarily personal and inescapably communal. It may seem that a preacher stands in the pulpit alone, but that is never actually the case. We are not meant to be lone voices in the wind. We are facilitating a dialogue between God's voice in scripture and the voice of God's people in worship. We are meant to stand in the middle, even as we stand in the front.

The traditional paradigm of preacher as sage-prophet-priest has done us a disservice. It makes it seem as if *I* have to be the expert, *I* have to dismantle abusive systems of power, *I* am responsible for tending to the cries of the people. Yes, each preacher does have a personal responsibility in all of those things, and we have each been given a unique and essential voice that has its own singular value, but we must tune that voice to lead the melody of a song that is actually being sung by a multitude of voices.

Thus, the call to preach is a call that cannot be answered in isolation. It requires the help of other faithful sojourners on a common journey to develop our priestly, prophetic, and sage-like imaginations. In so doing, the limitations of our individual perspectives are constructively challenged through the wisdom of communal discernment toward God's grace and justice at work in both the voice of scripture and the voices of God's people longing for the coming Kingdom. Perhaps the most remarkable Good News of the gospel's claim on us is that we are not called to do justice by ourselves, nor could we ever hope to do so. Whether standing in the pulpit or sitting in the pew, worshiping in the sanctuary or serving in the public square, Christians today join with the scriptural ancestors of our faith in serving as agents of the exceedingly abundant work God has already done, is doing, and will continue to do according to the gospel power that is at work in us.

Preachers Need Prophetic Community

In the preaching institute I direct at Fuller Theological Seminary, our vision is to catalyze a movement of empowered, wise preachers who do justice, love mercy, and walk humbly with God (Micah 6:8). Our primary vehicle for doing so is a program called Micah Groups, a multiethnic, transdenominational movement of preachers and church leaders who have been leading the church to address pressing issues of justice since 2011.[2]

When Micah Group preachers gathered in 2022, the conversation was quite different than it was when we began more than a decade ago. After the killing of Trayvon Martin in 2012, the thought of speaking about it from the pulpit had not occurred to a great many of our preachers outside the Black Protestant tradition, and many of our Black preachers reported never before having opportunity to dialogue about such prevalent injustice with non-Black clergy in a trusted setting. In 2022, it was inconceivable that any of our Micah Group preachers might not grasp the moral and spiritual claim that Black Lives Matter makes on our lives, pulpits, and congregations. Indeed, the pain and the blessing of recent years is that the depths of the fractures within American society have been inescapably revealed, and perhaps most notably, the unveiling of the fact that so many of the distorted beliefs at the heart of this fracturing—white supremacy, xenophobia, misogyny, Christian nationalism, to name but a few—have not only been tolerated in our preaching but have been enabled by it. As the prophet

Micah did in his time, we believe that leaders are needed in our time to call the church to repentance and help facilitate its restoration, even as we invite others to participate in God's Kingdom vision of a just society.[3]

While this is not a new vision for Micah Groups, it feels like a new season in the life of the universal church, and certainly of the American Christian church. In response, Micah Groups today seek to encourage a prophetic imagination among preachers by cultivating prophetic community. We are not particularly interested in promoting an approach to "prophetic preaching" per se but to preacher formation that includes mutual surrender to and discernment by a prophetic community in which diverse perspectives about the movement of God's grace in scripture, in the church, and in the public square will empower and equip our preaching and leadership.

This prophetic, communal formation is far more than an opportunity to develop homiletical skills or expand our voice and vision. It is also a commitment to accountability and solidarity with one another as we wrestle with the particular burden of a call to preach.

Preaching Is Precarious

Pastors today face what many feel is an unprecedented level of stress, isolation, and burnout. According to a March 2022 Barna study, 42 percent of pastors were considering quitting full-time ministry, with 38 percent of that group naming their reason as "current political divisions."[4] If preachers fear that a sermon declaring the authority of scripture will be deemed "too Republican" or a sermon advocating justice "too Democrat," or that mere mention of Black Lives Matter or COVID-19 or prayers for refugees will elicit "Your sermons are too political" backlash, then it is no great wonder why many are seeking an escape hatch. Indeed, such fear is about far more than discovering a few disgruntled emails on Monday morning. Anglican priest Tish Harrison Warren reflected on the situation in the *New York Times*, saying:

> Pastors bear not only their own pain but also the weight of an entire community's grief, divisions and anxieties. They are charged with the task of continuing to love and care for even those within their church who disagree with them vehemently and vocally. These past years required them to make decisions they were not prepared for that affected the health and spiritual formation of their community, and any decisions they made would likely mean that someone in their church would feel hurt or marginalized.[5]

Does any of this resonate with you? I certainly know many pastors who have felt crushed under the burdens of the recent past, and I know others who have been energized by an opportunity to try new experiments and have permission to innovate. Wherever you may find yourself and your ministry at this moment, it cannot be denied that the vocation of preaching is an often painful and always precarious call at any time, and even more so in the kind of climate we find ourselves today. That is, if we are doing it right.

Authentic proclamation of the Good News requires walking in the valley of human brokenness even as we point to the peak of God's grace. A sermon must work simultaneously to elicit confession of the broken human condition, acceptance of the healing balm of grace, and commitment to obedient discipleship. I don't know any way to do this without embracing Warren's sentiment that "pastors bear not only their own pain but also the weight of an entire community's grief, divisions and anxieties." We are being asked for answers we cannot provide, and yet we cannot ignore the questions.

Preachers Need a Learning Community

As a professor of preaching, I find that many of my students come to class believing they must somehow figure out how to write a sermon with all the right answers. To that end, they look to me for manuals and guidebooks, lists of instructions, templates, and rubrics to guide their sermon preparation. If the act of preaching were merely about delivering an entertaining message with a scriptural punchline and a spiritual action item, then sending students away with a handy just-add-water-and-mix sermon preparation plan might work. But the call to preach is not a call to write a sermon. It is a call to faithful leadership and discipleship that facilitates a community's embrace of the gospel's call to love God and neighbor, by which we seek together to do justice, love mercy, and walk humbly with God.

Thus, to many of my students' chagrin, my goal as a professor is not to help them accumulate a bag of tricks for ease in sermon writing, but rather to help instill habits that will aid a lifetime of preacher formation—within whatever community they may be called to serve, and among a global community of preaching peers who collectively witness to the bountiful abundance of God's love and justice. My hope is for each class to be a supportive, encouraging, and collaborative learning community where students emerge with new, or renewed, confidence, courage, and creativity as preachers.

Perhaps ironically, I am most often tasked with facilitating these learning communities in classes that are entirely online and asynchronous, with students from around the country and often from around the world. When Fuller Seminary created its first all-online MDiv degree option in 2018, I wondered how you could possibly teach preaching without meeting together face-to-face. Even if you could, it surely could not be effective. I was wrong. So wrong.

Online pedagogy is a very different approach, to be sure. If you've ever taken an Intro to Homiletics course, I wonder if it was anything like my own student experience—earnestly crafting a sermon for the benefit of your classmates and professor (or more likely, classmates and teaching assistant), that was delivered from a makeshift pulpit at the front of a classroom. There are certainly many benefits to this approach (and I dare say it turned out pretty okay for my classmates and me). However, I have found that my online students progress further and faster than my residential students, which I credit to their participation in a flourishing digital learning community that accompanies them as they practice the craft of preaching in real-world settings rather than sterile classroom labs.[6]

As it turns out, this model is not so different from the manner in which the Micah Groups program seeks to nurture and equip empowered, wise preachers who are already well-established in their preaching ministries. Micah Group members become part of a prophetic community of preachers longing to learn and grow together as they support, challenge, and encourage the craft of preaching and continual formation of the preacher in real-world settings. The key for both these learning communities is that all come to the table with open-handed vulnerability, ready to see themselves in new ways through the eyes of their peers.

You may not have the time or opportunity to join a formally organized preacher peer group, but there are other ways to work toward an ongoing posture of vulnerable curiosity and ongoing formation as a community of learners. One of these is to develop a lifelong habit of soliciting and reflecting on feedback.

PRAXIS — Preaching Feedback

Preaching Feedback in the Classroom

Learning to give and receive sermon feedback is perhaps the greatest gift of a seminary homiletics class, and yet it is often the most daunting aspect of the course. Opening oneself to critique is incredibly difficult because it is quite likely you will hear something you do not want to hear or are not ready to hear. This is where the movement of the Holy Spirit is of vital importance, so we must approach the feedback process with prayerful hearts and open minds as we grow into a community of trust and respect.

In my online courses, students preach to a Listening Group of at least five adults in their local context, then upload videos of their sermons for review by the class. Some students are already preaching in ministry settings, so they build the sermon assignments into their usual worship responsibilities, while others seek out friends and family to be their listeners. In either case, students learn to exegete their listeners' context together with the text at hand. They wrestle with what one particular thing, from one particular text, must be said to this particular community in this particular moment. They learn how to stand in the middle, even as they prepare to stand in the front.

After each sermon, students receive feedback from three sources: their local Listening Group, their seminary classmates, and me, their professor. Listeners are asked to comment solely on their own experience of the sermon with questions, such as "What did you find most encouraging about the message of this sermon?" and "What did this sermon help you understand about scripture?" Classmates are asked to offer constructive critique, commenting on the student preacher's engagement with scripture, theology, and listeners' context, as well as more practical concerns like the organization of the sermon or use of body and voice.

My feedback to students includes the requisite professorial attention to academic expectations, but beyond that, I am listening for each student's unique voice. Yes, I want to see curious and thorough exegesis, a compelling hermeneutic, and a well-structured presentation, but I also want to hear it through that preacher's authentic voice. As I watch each sermon, I am praying for the preacher and asking, "How is the Holy Spirit speaking through *you*?"

The feedback they receive from listeners and classmates is inevitably biased by those listeners' expectations for what a sermon "should" sound like. I am certainly not immune to those biases myself, but as I prayerfully seek out the particular voice of this particular preacher to this particular listening community, I hope that I can encourage them toward greater authority and authenticity in the way they have been designed to preach, which is likely a good bit different than the way I would do it.

All of this varied feedback from varied sources then must be prayerfully considered by the student. They have received *a lot* of feedback. While it can certainly be overwhelming, the goal is to build an understanding of what kinds of reflection will be most helpful throughout a lifetime preacher journey. That means this final stage of the process—where students must decide what to hold onto and what to let go—is really the most critical. Admittedly, I am frustrated when I see a student ignore what I consider to be the most important opportunities for their growth, but in the end, it's their own self-assessment (fueled by the Holy Spirit) that is far more important than my opinion about what they should do next.

Even beyond the pragmatic growth encouraged by this feedback process, students learn how to serve and be served by one another. They learn that giving feedback to another's sermon is just as vulnerable as receiving it for their own. This leads to more pastorally effective communication that arises from a desire for growth among the whole community, far beyond their own personal achievements.

Preaching Feedback in Ministry

Outside of a seminary classroom, preachers often find themselves feeling isolated, harried by the relentless pace of Sunday coming every week, and struggling to meet all the demands on their time—not least preparing each week's sermon. For many, the idea of finding time to engage in opportunities for formal, constructive feedback may seem ridiculous, if not impossible, considering the pressing demands of pastoral ministry that already leave precious little time for sermon preparation. It is certainly possible, though, to cultivate a more informal kind of learning community among preacher friends and peers, and even within your own congregation.

In my own preaching, I try to find regular opportunities for feedback from the same three sources that my students experience: listeners within the congregation, fellow preachers who can provide more constructive feedback through collegial conversation, and one or two trusted mentors who know me well and help me stay true to my own authentic voice.

We all have plenty of listeners, most of whom would love to give some feedback if given the opportunity. Having questions at the ready about how a person experienced that day's sermon can help solicit some casual feedback every week. For example, when a church member stops to say, "Good sermon, Pastor," what might happen if you respond, "I wonder, what did you find most encouraging about the message today?" Or perhaps, "I'm so glad it was meaningful for you. Is there anything in particular you are thinking about as a result?"

Questions such as these can help the preacher learn how their listeners are receiving a message and whether particular aspects resonate more strongly than others. It is also not uncommon to find that what a congregation member heard is not what the preacher actually said! Sometimes opening a dialogue is an opportunity for clarification, but more often it is simply a practice of continual exegesis of your listening community in order to learn what they are most attuned to hear. It may also help train the congregation to be better listeners, knowing that they will have a chance to discuss what they've taken in. Questions within the sermon itself can further encourage this: "You know, this is a really important concept for us to keep thinking about together. I'm going to ask you during the coffee hour what questions this raises for you, so be ready!"

Now that a majority of churches are streaming or posting worship videos online, it seems many of us look to number of views or number of likes as a barometer for the quality of a sermon. A spike or drop in views may, indeed, be an indication of something going on, but without more information, it's not particularly helpful feedback. Perhaps a change in numbers is an opportunity to practice vulnerable curiosity by sending the sermon link to a friend or peer from outside the usual worshiping community and inviting a conversation. Consider, for example, a periodic sermon exchange among preachers in your local denominational region or city pastors association.

Seeking new insights may also be helpful as part of a semi-yearly check-in or when experimenting with something new or different. Some pastors invite two or three elders, staff members, or other congregants to be part of a sermon talkback group for a season of time. I also know pastors who find it useful to distribute a survey to everyone in the congregation once or twice a year.

Lastly, a preaching mentor is a tremendous gift at every stage of your preaching vocation. This need not be a laborious process. Think about those preachers whom you admire and whose preaching resonates with you in a way that feels somehow familiar to your own style and sensibilities—or the opposite, someone whose preaching challenges you in a way that feels uncomfortable but also beneficial. Ask them to view and discuss with you one sermon a month for the next three months, or simply to have coffee once a quarter to exchange ideas. Both experienced and emerging preachers benefit greatly from these kinds of informal mentoring relationships. For me, occasions to serve as a mentor are equally edifying to those when I am the mentee, and I know many other preachers who feel similarly. So don't hesitate to make the ask.

Whatever method you may choose, the key is learning to ask the questions for which you most need to hear the answers, and to which you are actually ready to listen. (See the "Listening to Feedback" resource in *Appendix B* for some tips.)

In Micah Groups, we believe that readying ourselves to really listen—not only to what we think our preaching is saying, but also to how our preaching is being received—is a critical step toward embracing preaching within a prophetic community:

Every sermon is ultimately working toward calling out a response from people, but we need to take a searching and honest inventory of what response our preaching is truly working toward: Is it to comfort, to appease, to challenge, to see money in the offering plate, to be celebrated as a good preacher? Despite our best intentions, the wrong motivations easily, and continually, sneak in because, inevitably, preachers are consumed with one question—How do I keep people engaged? (i.e., How do I keep people entertained?)

We need to continually probe our own preaching for what we're really doing. We have to work through our issues about how much we want people to like us, or how afraid we are to lose people or financial contributions or even our job. If we are unable to confront these very personal fears, then we will be unable to confront the power of the empire, and our desire to do justice will be an empty one.[7]

Conclusion

We are called to be a plural *you* church. We are called to life in the community of the Body of Christ. As preachers, our role is to be facilitators of this community. We facilitate a dialogue between the people gathered and the many ways in which the grace of the Lord Jesus Christ, the love of God, and the communion of the Holy Spirit are with us all. Understanding that the gospel is a gospel of justice means we understand that all means *all*.

All means a community that draws the circle wide—around those we love and those who are very hard to love, around those who are known to us and those who are unknown. These are circles that grow continually larger, which we say is what we want because we want our churches to grow. But all too often, we aren't actually drawing a wider, larger circle. Instead, we try to attract more and more small circles— the kind that look and act the way we recognize and prefer. Small circles are so much more manageable.

The temptation as preachers is to be managers rather than facilitators: Manage the expectations of the congregation, manage the responsibilities of keeping the lights on, manage the boundaries that help us function. These are, of course, all functions of the job, but managers bear this weight alone, even as they delegate tasks to others. Alternatively, facilitators share the responsibility with the community, naming the reality of the situation and equipping a collective, communal response.

Preachers do not carry the burden of the gospel alone, nor do we rejoice in its Good News as individuals. We are asked to find our way into the text as we dwell among the people. Our minds and hands are open, waiting to be filled with the wisdom and movement of the Spirit. This makes us incredibly vulnerable. This makes us utterly human.

SERMON | Embodied Community | Acts 2:37–47

Rev. Inés Velásquez-McBryde
(former Fuller Seminary Chaplain;
Co-Lead Pastor of The Church We Hope For in Pasadena, CA)
Fuller Seminary Chapel—October 7, 2020
Available via Podcast or on YouTube[8]

> Awe came upon everyone because many wonders and
> signs were being done through the apostles. All who
> believed were together and had all things in common;
> they would sell their possessions and goods and
> distribute the proceeds to all, as any had need. Day by
> day, as they spent much time together in the temple,
> they broke bread at home and ate their food with glad
> and generous hearts, praising God and having the
> goodwill of all the people. And day by day the Lord
> added to their number those who were being saved.
> — ACTS 2:43–47

In October 2020, worship at Fuller Seminary—like so many places—was entirely online due to the COVID-19 pandemic. Our all-seminary chapel services were interactive communal gatherings held on Zoom and streamed to additional worshipers joining through other online platforms. In such a setting as this, it may seem ironic to hear a sermon on "Embodied Community," but that is precisely what we all tried to practice as we brought our individual bodies from individual places, spread around the world, into one united community of worship.

At the start of each Zoom service of worship, Chapel Director Julie Tai invited all gathered to light a candle. This simple act of invocation helped remind us that the office, living room, or kitchen table where we sat was actually sacred space. As flames began to flicker in each Zoom screen, all those individual sacred spaces became one community.

Fuller Seminary is a multilingual campus, with classes offered in Korean and Spanish as well as English, and so our chapel services include multilingual elements. This service also happened to occur during Hispanic Heritage Month, so the liturgy and preaching flowed seamlessly back and forth between English and Spanish. This was an opportunity not only to celebrate Hispanic heritage, but also to celebrate a bilingual life. The unilingual speakers among us were encouraged to try not to tune out when a different language was being spoken, but rather to lean in even more. As Julie advised, "The Holy Spirit has a way of communicating to us even in languages that we don't commonly use in our day to day."

Into this worship space where all were separated by geography, and many by language, Pastora Inés Velásquez-McBryde invited us to join together in the vision of embodied community from Acts 2 by gathering at her abuela's mesa:

> *Esta mañana quiero invitarles a la mesa de mi abuela y como ella encarnó los valores de la nueva familia en los vv. 44–47. La nueva familia aquí suena y huele como la sopa de frijoles de mi abuela.*

> *This morning I'd like to invite you to my abuela's mesa, my grandmother's table, and how she embodied the principles of this nueva familia in vs. 43–47. The new community here, which I will refer to as Nueva Familia, sounds and smells like my abuela's Nicaraguan Black Bean Soup.*

Throughout this sermon—and in every bilingual sermon she is called upon to preach—Inés begins with the Spanish first because it disrupts the patterns of our English-centered imaginations. This is an intentional embodiment in her homiletics that requires listeners to tune their ears in a new way. Like the believers gathered at Pentecost in Acts 1, we are invited to gather in a new kind of community, where a Spirit-driven disruption of power demands that one language will not be privileged over another.

Inés takes care, however, to ensure that the disruption of language is not a disruption of hospitality. She beckons all listeners into her abuela's kitchen via thick descriptions that allow us to imagine joining in the soup making process and picking the rocks out of the dried beans on the table, *"God forbid you bit into one of those rocks while eating!"*

I am not Nicaraguan, I do not speak Spanish, and I have never spent three days making soup, but almost immediately in this sermon, I feel that I am part of this family. I feel welcome in this abuela's kitchen. Inés has not yet told us how this relates to Acts 2, but she has shown us. She has demonstrated through storytelling what it could look like to be a community of people who break bread with glad and generous hearts, praising God, and having the goodwill of all people.

The nueva familia in these verses didn't happen overnight. This nueva familia is a response of the hearts broken by the work of Jesus on the cross and the movement of the Spirit among them. Verse 37 says that they were "cut to the heart" and asked that provocative question, "What should we do?"

Now we are in the text. The *nueva familia* described in Acts is a product of God's love, established through the utmost grace and devotion of Christ's redemption and the Holy Spirit's sustenance. Now we are hearing Good News.

Three thousand believers responded to this Good News in communal repentance (vv. 38–41). *Could it be that they realized not only how they had sinned against God but also how sin had kept them from each other?* We miss the power of Pentecost if we read

Acts 2 as a call to individual repentance. This is a call to community. This is a call to love not only God, but also neighbor. This is a call to share our soup.

This was a Spirit-spoken story where the Spirit is the Story-Maker and the people are the Story-Tellers. I can't help but hear this as a preacher, and as a call to preach. The gospel is a Spirit-spoken story where the Spirit is the Story-Maker and preachers are called to be the Story-Tellers. We are a community of Story-Tellers. Tellers of the Gospel (capital G) Story (capital S). Of course, you don't have to be a preacher to tell this Story, which seems to be the point Inés is making here. We have been baptized into a communal Story, and we share in telling that Story through our very lives.

This is a Border-Crossing God with a Boundary-Breaking Spirit, bringing together those who otherwise would not have eaten together before. This Story goes so far beyond the margins of our individual pages. This is an incredible declaration of the Good News—we are loved by a God who breaks boundaries on our behalf. Our work is not to be the breakers, but simply to be the gatherers. We are to follow the Spirit's beckoning across borders and boundaries, gathering as part of a community that looks and sounds and behaves differently than we had imagined while stifled behind the boundaries of our own making.

These are the very boundaries to which Inés turns next. Recall the newspaper headlines of October 2020—most of the world sent home to quarantine from COVID-19, anti-Asian hate and violence on the rise, Black Lives Matter protests in the streets, and an intensely polarized election about to take place.

If I were to rewrite verses 44–47, and with newspaper in hand, it would say this: All who believed were divided and demonizing the other. They had nothing in common any-more. They hoarded toilet paper during a global pandemic and hoarded resources that could otherwise help the other. The thousands who were overcome by this virus showed how inequity was distributed among black and brown commu-nities. And if anyone had need and sought asylum at the border, they would be teargassed, turned away, or placed in detention centers. Children were dismembered from their mother's arms, and women that were left had their wombs pulled out. Day by day they spent less time listening to their lives' stories together. And with angry and cynical hearts, they ate alone, with no one else at their table with whom to share their soup.

Now we see ourselves in this story. The very uncomfortable "we" that some of us would rather not talk about because it is some-where "out there," far beyond our own kitchen table, while oth-ers have no table at which to rest. But Inés is not calling for individual repentance of personal failures, she is calling for a communal repentance. We must recognize the communal ways that we have failed one another, failed to gather around abuela's mesa. By placing our contemporary reality side-by-side with the vision of the text, Inés places us inside the biblical witness. The message is clear. We are failing to live as the church has been called.

Mi abuela's faithful steps were to feed bodies and to feed souls, because when our bodies are well, it is well with our soul. . . . Often Nicaraguan women in our church fed our community, soul food and real food, after earthquakes, hur-ricanes, and during the war.

We are invited to participate in the Acts vision of the Church by sharing our soup—literally and figuratively. Faith must be more than words, more than dogma. It must be lived, and it must be lived in community.

Earthquakes, hurricanes, wars, pandemics, systemic injustice are all far beyond our individual capacities to confront or solve or heal, but that is not our work. Our work is to practice hospitality and presence by tending to the bodies and souls right in front of us, or by allowing our own body and soul to be nurtured at someone else's abuela's mesa. This is the Good News at work within us.

> *Sharing your soup was the best sermon my abuela ever preached and taught me. This was a sign and wonder and a witness of the living presence of Jesus in our midst to me. . . . That embodied the power of the Cross in Ephesians where Jesus came to abolish in the flesh the enmity, and put to death the hostility, and out of two groups, created one new familia.*

> *My prayer is that my abuelita's mesa, and her theology of familia, would illuminate, inform, and form our different theological and social mesas and tables. That the promises of God would flow through the people of God and through the mesas that we set. This is a work of the Spirit to sit at Spirit-filled Mesas where the black bean soup is the aroma of Christ.*

This sermon is filled with the aroma of Christ. It is not a classically expository sermon, working point by point through the text, and yet it is firmly rooted in scripture. Inés's imagination, cultural context, and pastoral instincts made a way into the text that helped us see something new. She didn't help us see ourselves in the gathering of the early church in Acts, but instead to see ourselves gathering as the church in Acts today.

Remember, too, that this was a bilingual service for Hispanic Heritage month. For white, English-speaking listeners like me, gathering at abuela's mesa was a novel idea that inspired me to think about the church in new ways and challenged me to confront my privileged assumptions about what the church *should* be. For Hispanic listeners, I imagine this was a comforting message of hope and assurance that, despite what Western Christianity may be saying about what the church should be, the Spirit is doing a mighty work at their very own mesas.

Inés never said the word "justice," but it was there. Proclaiming the Good News of a border-crossing, boundary-breaking God orients us to a gospel of justice that upends worldly notions of power and safety and individualism, calling us instead to lives of repentance, hospitality, and community. This is very Good News indeed.

CHAPTER 2

A Covenant of Justice

"With what shall I come before the Lord
and bow myself before God on high?
Shall I come before him with burnt
offerings, with calves a year old?
Will the Lord be pleased with thousands of
rams, with ten thousands of rivers of oil?
Shall I give my firstborn for my transgression,
the fruit of my body for the sin of my soul?"
He has told you, O mortal, what is good,
and what does the Lord require of you
but to do justice and to love kindness and
to walk humbly with your God?
— MICAH 6:6–8

Micah 6:8 is the quintessential justice verse in scripture. Count-less eponymous programs and organizations have claimed it as a theme verse and mandate, including the Micah Groups preacher formation program that I direct. Our mission is to catalyze a movement of empowered, wise preachers who do justice, love mercy, and walk humbly with God, leading others to join God's mission in the world. We hold this prophetic cry of Micah to be a requirement not only for our own personal lives and spiritual formation, but also to be the vision for our leadership in the church—the Body of Christ that God has called to be an instrument of reconciliation and justice in our fractured world. The power of Micah 6:8 cannot be fully understood, however, when extracted from its context within Micah's broader prophetic mandate.

At this moment in biblical history, Israel is in pretty bad shape. They are dealing with corrupt rulers, false prophets, and idolatry everywhere they turn. And—spoiler alert—in the end, Israel does not heed Micah's urging to change their ways, and they are conquered by the Assyrians. It's really no surprise that it ends this way, because as we can see here in Micah 6, they really are not getting it. Their rhetorical questions say it all.

I love questions. I like to ask questions. I'm very curious. I like to know how things work and how people think and how one thing leads to the next. There are people in my life who don't really appreciate the number of questions that I ask because they feel pressured to come up with satisfactory answers. Often, though, my questions are not really about finding answers. Good questions lead to other questions, which become an ongoing dialogue that helps us grow deeper in relationship.

There is one question, however, that I find absolutely, completely unacceptable. If you really want to get to know me, you won't get very far by asking, "So . . . what's new with you?" To me, this is a bad question. It's a lazy question. It's a question that says, "I'm willing to sit here and give you my time, but you have to do the work. You tell me what I should be interested in. You tell me what might be entertaining to me."

If you ask, "What's new with your job?" you've told me something about my life that interests you and that we can dialogue about. "What's new with your family?" tells me something else. "What's new with you?" tells me: "You stay over there; I'll stay over here. We checked in. Everything's fine. I can go on with my life, and you can go on with yours." Real relationship requires good questions, questions that reveal something about ourselves as the question asker, not just the question answerer.

In this passage, Israel's opening question is very revealing—they don't get it. *With what shall I come before the Lord and bow myself before God on high?* This question is dripping with sarcasm. They're actually asking, "What do I have to do, God, to get you off my back?" They aren't invested in this relationship in the same way that God is.

This question reminds me of those moments when you walk into the room with someone you know very well—whether it's your spouse or child or coworker or friend—and you feel an icy chill in the room. It's clear something is not right here, but what? Is it about me? Am I in trouble? This moment requires a really good connecting question like, "Would you like to talk?" or "How can I help?" A moment like this calls for a question that draws us deeper into the complexity, but all too often we are looking for an escape hatch and turn instead to very unhelpful questions like, "What is your problem?" or "What do you want from me?!"

Israel has walked into the icy chill of Yahweh's displeasure, and they respond with the worst kind of question. It's a defensive, sarcastic question that says, "I recognize that something is going on here, but you keep it over there, and I'll continue with my life the way I like it over here, thank you very much."

Micah has been telling Israel what's going on—and telling them, and telling them, and telling them. They've become more and more corrupt with greed and occult practices, with worship of idols, and they're separating themselves as they fall deeper and deeper into sinful ways. Micah is trying desperately to pull them back into communion with God, and they're saying, "Ugh, fine, what do I have to bring? How about my calves, my lambs, my oil? Oh, I know, let me give you my firstborn child. Is that good enough for you? Will that appease you so we can just get on with it?"

Then Micah asks a better question: *"What does the Lord require of you?"* This is a very different question than, "What should I bring to the Lord?" This is, "What is required of *you?*" Not something else, but *you.*

And what does the Lord require of you—O mortal—but to do justice, to love kindness, and to walk humbly with God? These things are all about being in relationship; all about how we dwell in communion with one another and with God. It's not about giving *things*. It's about bringing ourselves.

Now, I don't have calves or rams or oil. I don't have any children. I can't give any of this stuff to God. But I try to make this deal with God all the time. I say, "Look, God, I gave you all my money, my time, my work. I've got student loan debt from the education that made me a pastor so that I can actually do justice. My entire job is about helping other pastors do justice, teaching students to think about justice, and preaching to congregations about justice. My life is justice, justice, justice. See, I'm doing it all for you, God. Isn't that enough?!"

And God says to me, "Oh *mortal*. I require you. I require *you*." I'm doing the work, I'm checking it off my list, but when am I actually drawing nearer to God? When am I walking slowly, humbly? When am I showing mercy? When do I stop to ask better questions?

The requirement of Micah 6:8 is an orienting of our entire lives around the character of God. God requires nothing less of us than is already being given to us. Justice is the work God is doing in our world to upend wrongly ordered power, an effort that we join by walking with humility to see God's power at work far above and beyond our own, and all of this is made possible because of God's steadfast love for us—God's fundamental nature of *hesed*.

Beginning preaching students love to quote Greek and Hebrew in their sermons. For many of us newly embracing the wonders of exegetical discovery, it seems like unlocking a magic decoder ring, and we want to bestow all of this fascinating minutiae on our listeners. To the average listener, however, it's generally a distraction from whatever is the primary focus of the text and the hermeneutic at hand. The one exception, I tell my students, is when the word in the original language is so important, and so thoroughly impossible to define in the language of your listeners, that you actually want everyone to learn this exact word. For me, *hesed* is one of these exceptions.

English translations for *hesed* refer to "loving kindness" or "steadfast mercy." In the case of Micah 6:8, we are told that enacting *hesed* means to love mercy or to love kindness. None of this gets to the heart of the matter, though. These words in English are not nearly powerful enough. They do not come close to carrying the weight of *hesed*. God's very being is *hesed*, reflecting not only self-sacrificing love but also faithfulness, kindness, generosity, grace, and fiercely devoted loyalty that is expressed to Israel—and to us—in the most extraordinary ways.

Hesed is covenantal. *Hesed* is unchanging. *Hesed* is the kind of love that is mostly unimaginable to us because there is no equal in our human experience. We misunderstand Micah's requirement if we approach it as something we must do to appease God—something we must do to be a good Christian, or for that matter, a good human. In fact, the only reason we have any ability to meet this requirement in the first place is because God has already done, is doing, and will continue to do justice for us, to extend unending love and mercy to us, to walk with us in the humble power and authority of Christ. This is the extraordinarily amazing Good News of the gospel!

We are called upon merely to reflect back to God all that has first been extended to us. The call to love God and neighbor is a call to do justice simply (but certainly not easily) by living into a joyful, unconditional, bilateral covenant relationship, which is a good bit different than a tit-for-tat sense of obligation. From here, we are poised to ask much better questions:

God of Grace, where will our hurting world find healing?
Lord of Light, what do I need to see more clearly?
Holy Spirit, how are you moving in our midst and asking me to participate?

God has created us for communion—communion with the Father, Son, and Spirit, and communion with one another. Communion is about mutual delight—delight with the Lord, delight with one another, and even delight in ourselves. When I choose to rest in this sense of delight rather than a sense of obligation, I begin to see outside my self-centered inclinations and toward the well-being of my neighbor. From here, using my gifts for ministry and service become the natural outpouring from the ever-expanding desires of my heart for God and for others. Suddenly, a commitment to do justice is no longer a burden but another form of blessing.

The most *hesed*-like desire of God is to partner with us in this kind of justice-seeking, mercy-loving, humble dance of life.

Justice Preaching Is Good News

My approach to preaching, and the premise of this book, is that every sermon is a proclamation of the gospel, which means every sermon is a call to justice. Many preachers will surely disagree with this compulsory link between gospel and justice. "Every sermon should declare personal forgiveness through Christ," one such preacher told me recently. Certainly, this is a hallmark of the gospel that warrants significant homiletical exploration, but it isn't separate from or counter to a gospel of justice. Quite the opposite, I'd say. The Good News of forgiveness through Christ is precisely what sets us free to shape our hearts and minds around participating in a counter-cultural community of faith that seeks justice.

A vision for preaching that avoids the gospel's call to justice is simply too small. It lays claim on only one piece of the gospel's promise. It happily declares, "Repent and be baptized," but not "Feed my sheep." It diminishes the power of the cross by suggesting the gift of Christ's death and resurrection is to pass out tickets to heaven. This is another way we get stuck in the myopia of an individualistic discipleship. When we read the gospels through the lens of community, we can't help but see the incarnation, life, death, and resurrection of Jesus Christ as a cataclysmic reordering of unjust power.

Jesus declares he has come to fulfill the law of the prophets, and whoever breaks these laws—and teaches others to do the same—"will be called least in the kingdom of heaven"; whoever follows these laws—and teaches others to do the same—"will be called great in the kingdom of heaven" (Matthew 5:17–19). Our participation in the Kingdom depends on our engagement with Christ's teaching through participation with others. The Kingdom of Heaven is a community in which the law of God is fulfilled for and among all the people of God.

This is made abundantly clear when Jesus is asked, "What must I do to inherit eternal life?" and his answer is, "You shall love the Lord our God with all your heart, and with all your soul, and with all your strength, and with all your mind; and you shall love your neighbor as yourself" (Luke 10:25–27). Eternal life is not a singular proposition. Eternal life is commitment to a guiding ethos of neighbor-love, through which our desires for others are to be at least as much as we desire for ourselves. This suggests respect, generosity, reciprocity, and equity. Loving your neighbor is doing justice.

The cross represents the very worst our world has to offer—the result of an unjust, corrupt, abusive system that oppresses and marginalizes any threat to the empire. Jesus bore this suffering of a world in agony and showed us that it is not the end of our story. Through Christ's resurrection there is hope for a new kingdom, a new creation, a new world order where God's *hesed* is most fully manifest.

Proclaiming a gospel of justice is not solely about the literary Gospels of Matthew, Mark, Luke, and John. God's heart for justice and call for our participation in it pervades the entire canon of scripture. The message of the New Testament epistles further defines a working theology for the ministry of the church as the Body of Christ—a Body called to be neighbor-lovers, who are no longer Gentile or Jew, slave or free, woman or man, but are all one in Christ (Galatians 3).

The message of the Old Testament helps us learn from God's relationship with the people of Israel—a people who were continually being rescued, shaped, molded, and formed as a community living according to the great I Am's covenant of *hesed*. The law, the prophets, and wisdom literature all agree that the upholding of this covenant means jumping into God's everflowing stream of justice and righteousness (Amos 5) by responding to the great requirement of being people of justice, mercy, and humility (Micah 6).

Collectively, all of this is the Good News that makes it possible for us to participate in God's ongoing work of justice. All too often, though, I find myself listening to so-called "justice sermons" that seem to leave out the Good News altogether. I've heard stirring calls to action around racial reconciliation, creation care, immigration advocacy, LGBTQ+ rights, and so much more. Often, I am in complete agreement with the message, and perhaps I can readily imagine a biblical theology to support it, but the preacher has not actually proclaimed one. When students offer such messages in my preaching courses, I find myself giving feedback such as, "This was a wonderful creation care speech for Earth Day, but it was not a sermon."

Sermons must point first to what God is already doing in the world, and second to how we are able to join in that work. The only way our efforts in racial reconciliation, immigration advocacy, or any other socio-political concern will truly be acts of justice is when those efforts are joined with God's acts of justice already in progress.

Furthermore, messages centered primarily in justice advocacy rather than biblical theology are very often preaching to the choir—they are rallying calls for a community already poised toward progressive social action. Don't we also want to bring those for whom "justice" is a dirty word drummed up by the liberal media into an understanding of the gospel as justice? Confronting those listeners with a list of action items toward social justice reform is alienating. Our polarized congregations first need to be brought into an understanding of God's heart for justice, which will help us move nearer to the heart of God and, in so doing, begin to imagine how God's grace and forgiveness and mercy are all part of a communal call to participate in God's will being done on earth, as it is in heaven.

We all need to be reminded of the extent to which we are loved and cherished by a benevolent God. We are loved by a God who beckons us to do better, to be better, but even when we fail to do so, continues to hold and cherish and nurture us. Justice sermons (and again, I believe every sermon is a call to justice in one form or another) are most effective when they begin by expressing what God is already doing for us—what God is doing in the world that we may need to see differently or more vividly. We need to hear preachers name the myriad ways in which we all experience the love and grace and justice and mercy of God, *and then* how we are called to respond. Leaning into the Good News becomes a natural way to ask a very good question: "How can we love more like God loves?"

How can we possibly succeed in answering a call to go out into the world as justice people if we aren't being fed already and nourished already from the love that we receive through the grace of God? The work of justice requires human participation, but it is only ever begun by divine initiation. Many of the sermons I have heard of late are 90 percent telling people how to think and what to do, and 10 percent how Jesus can help you do that. We need to flip this script. Not only will this be a more accurate representation of the gospel message, but it will also be more convincing. We've got to help people imagine why they should agree to take the yoke of Jesus upon them—because in this burden we find rest for our souls (Matthew 11:29–30).

Justice Preaching Is Scriptural

It seems to me that sermons straying away from proclamation and veering toward self-help talks or stump speeches tend to do so because they also stray away from scripture. For example, consider a creation care message that begins with a reading of Genesis 1 as a reason to declare "God loves creation and so should we," but the entirety of the sermon expounds on all the ways we have failed creation, and presents a five-point plan for doing better. Do we need to repent of our failure to be stewards of the earth? Absolutely. Can a sermon help us imagine a new way forward? Certainly. But it's all finger wagging and a potential bully pulpit exercise if the sermon never explores the manner in which God's love is poured out to us through the mystery of creation, or how God has provided for us through a symbiotic relationship with all living things, or what it means that we've been formed in the image of God, or what it means that the author of all creation would deign to give mere humans dominion. Our call to justice on behalf of the earth can only ever be in response to what God has already done, and to what God has called "good."

Many sermons include very good messages about how to be better humans, but when they are not rooted in the biblical text, they become entirely humanistic. To be fair, I don't believe most of such preaching intends to support secular humanism. Quite the contrary, it seems more often the result of deeply ingrained dogma about God's role in our world leading to an assumption that all of our listeners are on the same page. Much of the time, they are. And often, they are not. Either way, we've got to connect the dots—whether for the cradle Christian who needs to be reminded, or for the seeker hearing these ideas for the first time. Messages about what we are to do and to be, if not rooted in the text, are not as likely to fully root in our hearts because they are disconnected from the living, breathing Word.

Thus, our first task when preparing to preach is to mine the text in front of us, allowing the text to speak first and foremost, before any ideas or assumptions that may have brought us to this text in the first place. Of course, we want to have ideas. God wants our ideas. Our listeners need to hear our ideas. But it's a dance. Our ideas need to emanate from what the Holy Spirit is drawing us to hear from the voice of God spoken in scripture.

I am continually mystified by sermons that not only ignore what seems to me to be the most pertinent connections in scripture, but also do cartwheels around the text by substituting their own metaphors, parables, or narratives. Consider, for example, a sermon I heard recently on prayer, based on Matthew 6, that never once mentioned The Lord's Prayer. Jesus literally says, "This is how you are to pray," but we heard nothing of that. Instead, the preacher offered, "This is the way that I pray." The way the preacher prayed was actually quite a helpful example, but by jumping away from the text, we were never able to see what this had to do with the Good News of the relationship Jesus proclaims through the invitation to know God as "Our Father."

One Lent, I visited a church where a sermon on atonement began with a reading from Leviticus 16. "How brave!" I thought to myself, as I settled in to learn how Israel's seemingly anti-quated rituals of sacrifice might be relevant to our world today. Instead, the preacher deconstructed traditional systematic the-ologies of atonement, offering little, if any, biblical reflection (from Leviticus or elsewhere), and concluding with the confes-sion, "I'm still trying to figure this out. Maybe you are too. We don't need to agree, we just need to keep working on it together." This vulnerable authenticity is a laudable posture from the pul-pit, and the message that we are all struggling with the mysteries of our faith is an important one. But untethered from scripture's witness that God is at work, even if we see that work through a glass dimly, this is not Good News. Instead, I wonder if partner-ing theological deconstruction with an honest reckoning of the Law in Leviticus may have provided a framework for listeners to hold onto the Good News of the freedom from sin afforded to us, even while wrestling with the complicated and often prob-lematic theological assumptions of tradition.

All of this leads me to a growing conviction that we must dig deep into the text to consistently dwell in the Good News—the Good News of a justice-seeking God who is deeply concerned with the agonizing consequences of our inability to see clearly. We must carefully attune our senses toward the movement of the Holy Spirit to discover a hermeneutic that meets us on the ground in the particularities of our lives today. Then, and only then, the homiletical turn applies that hermeneutic in a way that our communities can integrate into a humble walk of merciful justice with God.

Preachers Need Good News

I wonder if one of the reasons it may be difficult to focus on Good News in our preaching is because we are so desperately in need of it ourselves. We are trying to be prophet, sage, and priest, but ordination or seminary education or sanctification by elders doesn't give us a magic wand to suddenly see or interpret truth any more clearly than the next person. First and foremost, we are disciples—just like every one of our listeners. We are exegeting the text to find a word for ourselves as much as for anyone else.

The importance of spiritual formation and maintaining habits of spiritual disciplines is certainly not an innovative idea. I know many preachers for whom these regular patterns of prayer, meditation, and abiding in the Word are as compulsory in their day as eating breakfast or brushing their teeth. That is not me. I wish it was. Alas, my patterns of formation are more akin to Jacob's wrestling with God.

I wrote an entire doctoral dissertation on the necessity of abiding in what I have called "Sacramental Silence," following the practices of Howard Thurman.[1] At some point well into the writing process, I found myself in a therapy session prattling on and on about Thurman's contributions, to which my therapist patiently (sarcastically?) mused, "Hmm, I wonder why you were drawn to write about Thurman. Could it be that you need such Sacramental Silence in your own life?" I was so busy writing and studying and researching and working and trying to call out these practices that I saw as formative for ministries of worship, preaching, and justice that I wasn't doing it myself.

46

Howard Thurman was a twentieth-century theologian, pastor, and academic who is perhaps most remembered as a contemplative and mystic who had a profound impact on the Civil Rights movement of the 1960s. As I immersed myself in Thurman's world, I came to see him walking in the dark void of silence forced upon a Black man in a white world, a sensitive soul in a harsh climate, a seeker of creativity and truth in a religion of dogma and certitude. The context of Thurman's contemplative spirituality, however, had shown him that it is not God who is silent but rather the world's unceasing brutality that attempts to silence God. In a contest of noise, the world's relentless discord will always win. Such insidious evil can be vanquished in only one way—by confidently and purposefully striding directly into the silence and finding that place where, as Thurman has put it, "God speaks without words and the self listens without ears."[2]

His own grappling with scripture led Thurman to put forth what was, for the time, a revolutionary theology: Jesus was not privileged; Jesus did not wield earthly power; Jesus was one of the disinherited with his "back against the wall"; and yet he lived in the liberating confidence of bearing the *imago Dei*.[3] Jesus developed this confidence of identity through his own divine encounters of Sacramental Silence, providing the agency needed to live his love-ethic as suffering servant. This is the example for all to follow. For the oppressed, it leads to reclamation of a God-given voice; for the oppressor, it leads to repentance for silencing God-given voices; for both, it requires steeping oneself in Sacramental Silence that makes way for God's voice to empower one's own.

Though regarded by many as the spiritual father of the Civil Rights movement, Thurman was not an activist in the same way as Martin Luther King, Jr., Vincent Harding, Jesse

Jackson, Rosa Parks, John Lewis, or any of the other very public advocates and protesters of the time. Thurman wasn't marching in the streets, but his footprints are clearly embedded in the spiritual sand because he was walking with Jesus and helping others do the same. Thurman preached the gospel of justice by living into its Good News with every part of his life. In so doing, "He gave us the basis for the march," reflects Otis Moss, Jr., "that we know why we march, the principles upon which we march, how we march, and what we do after the march."[4]

If any of us has any hope of proclaiming Good News in our sermons, we have to seek it, believe it, and claim it in our own lives. There will be doubts. There will be questions. There will be bouts with darkness and silence and absence. This is all part of the journey of discipleship we are each called to walk. Through our preaching we have the opportunity to model for others what it may look like to, as Thurman so eloquently suggests, "see the illumined finger of God" guiding our journey:

Against the darkness for the age I can see the illumined finger of God guiding me in the way that I should go, so that high above the clash of arms in the conflict for position, for rights, for status, for place, for priority, I can hear speaking distinctly and clearly to my own spirit the still small voice of God without which nothing has meaning, quite, with which all the rest of the journey, however difficult, however painful, however devastating will be filled with a music all its own and even the stars in their courses and all the wooded world of nature participate in the triumphant music of my heart.[5]

PRAXIS—Exegetical Journal

An exegetical journal is one of the tools I have found most helpful for sermon preparation that goes deep into scripture and encourages personal, spiritual reflection. This is the method that was presented to me as a homiletics student and the method I teach today.[6] It is also the method that continues to inform my own preaching preparation, although I no longer write all of it down. It has become a mostly internalized process that guides my study, reflection, and prayer in the days, and usually weeks, leading up to a sermon. (See *Appendix B* for an exegetical journal template and detailed explanation.)

The most important aspect of this process is to avoid doing all of the exegetical or preparatory work in one sitting. The text needs to steep in us over a period of time during which the Holy Spirit moves as we simply carry the text with us throughout our daily life. I realize this may sound absurd, or like a wishful luxury of time that few working preachers are allowed, but it need not be a laborious undertaking. In fact, I find that it actually reduces the amount of time I need to spend in front of a computer or surrounded by books. It is mostly a matter of planning ahead.

At least one week prior to preaching—select the sermon text. For regular, ongoing preaching, or anytime I am preaching more than one Sunday in a row, I usually develop a sermon series appropriate to the liturgical season and events in the life of the church. In that case, I will have committed to the sermon text several weeks or even months in advance. At this point, I have read the text several times, but have not invested any significant study time. Simply knowing that I've got a sermon coming up on John 6, for example, means that "I Am the Bread of Life" will be ringing in my ears.

At least three days before preaching—ask questions of the text. Come to the text with an open heart and mind, even if it is one with which you are very well acquainted. Read it several times, slowly, prayerfully. Lectio Divina is very helpful at this point. Get curious, ask questions, let your imagination roam free. Resist the urge to move too quickly to a specific sermon focus or title. Don't open commentaries or other study guides yet. Sit with your questions. Allow yourself space to wonder. Keep wondering as you drive to an appointment, wait in line at a store, or stand in the shower.

At least two days before preaching—study the text. Pursue answers to questions raised during your initial wondering time. Whenever possible, do your own exegetical study first, before turning to commentaries (or blogs!). Allow your own instincts and ideas to develop through consideration of literary and historical context, original language, parallel texts, and so forth. (For seasoned preachers, this is often accomplished by a review of previous notes or mental audit of the years of study already well ingrained.) Bring these ideas to your reading of commentaries to see what affirms or challenges your thinking, or what things you may have overlooked. Consult nonbiblical resources, such as literature, films, and podcasts, to put the text in dialogue with cultural context.

A note on bibliography: take a quick audit of books and resources to which you regularly turn. Who are the predominant voices you are listening to in your preparation? Are there women? Are there people of color? Is a range of ages represented? Are you reading anything written in the last five years? Do you read across a theological spectrum, rather than exclusively within your own tradition? If your go-to sources are fairly homogenous, it's time to find some new titles to add to your shelf.

Prior to writing your sermon—determine a central focus of the text. All of this exegetical wondering and studying is meant to allow the text to reveal a particular focus for this particular sermon. Every text will offer countless possible directions, but the strongest sermons are firmly rooted in only one. There are a number of methods to utilize here. You may be familiar, for example, with Thomas Long's "Focus and Function" or Haddon Robinson's "The Big Idea."[7] My preferred method is developing a "Core Affirmation," as set forth by Sally Brown and Luke Powery in their homiletics textbook *Ways of the Word.*[8]

For a sermon to proclaim the Good News of God's *hesed* call to justice, it has to have a central focus that both demonstrates God's heart for us and calls us to respond. We need to know—first—what God is already doing and—second—how we are to join in that doing. The Core Affirmation method ensures that both parts of this equation are central to the development of a sermon.

According to Brown and Powery, a Core Affirmation is a declarative sentence that will (1) "affirm some divine action that is either demonstrated, implied, or assumed in the text—something God (Father-Creator, incarnate Son, or Spirit) *has* done, *is* doing, or *promises to do*" and (2) "the difference this divine action makes in the world of human experience." This results in a statement like, *"Because God* has acted [is acting/ promises to act] in the following way—[therefore]—*we are able* to do the following. . ."[9]

My preaching students include a Core Affirmation in their exegetical journals following a brief summary of their concluding observations about the text. This means the journaling process acts as a kind of funnel, beginning with the broadest possible considerations, drawing in to more specific textual and contextual considerations, narrowing still further to a summary of key findings, and finally producing a clear, concise Core Affirmation for the sermon. I ask them to write their statement in *exactly* this way:

> *This sermon will declare that because God (has/is/ will)* _____,
> *We are (able to/called to/respond by)* _____
> _____.

I vigilantly enforce this specific wording because I believe it sets preachers up to succeed in a sermon that proclaims Good News and provides a direct application for what we do with Good News in our lives. Even so, I am surprised at how often students have a very difficult time calling out Good News. Instead, the "because God" part of the equation becomes a divine dictate rather than a divine action on our behalf. Core Affirmations along those lines look something like this:

- . . . because God wants us to love our neighbor, we respond by working for justice.
- . . . because God is testing our faith, we are called to show faith in our actions.
- . . . because God is calling us to be Kingdom citizens, we are able to be loving.

Well sure, but where's the part about how God has already loved us, already been faithful to us, already been doing justice for us? This is the gospel we must proclaim in every sermon. We stand to preach only *because God* has done a mighty work in our midst, and our listeners are longing to understand what the particular text at hand demonstrates about that mighty work.

Another Core Affirmation pitfall I encounter is being overly broad:

- . . . because God has loved us, we can love others.
- . . . because God has redeemed us, we are free.
- . . . because God is gracious, we can have doubts.

Do you have any idea what chapter and verse may have inspired any of those statements? Being redeemed and free, or loved and loving, or grace-filled and doubting could apply to virtually any biblical text in one way or another, and so they do little to focus a sermon on the particular call of one particular text. "God has loved us, so we can love others" might be a great theme statement to help a worship team choose music and liturgical elements, but a sermon needs richer and more specific language than that. I encourage the use of key words, images, or ideas that have come from the text itself. For example, each of the following Core Affirmations is about God loving us so we can love others, but is more specific to the particularities of the text at hand:

- *A sermon on 1 John 4:* . . . because God's very essence is love, which is extended to us at our birth, we are called to love others so God's love can be perfected in us.
- *A sermon on Romans 8:* . . . because God, through Christ, has loved us beyond the power of death or any force of creation, we are able to live free of condemnation, extending the same freeing love to others.

- *A sermon on Micah 6:* . . . because God loves us according to his fundamental nature of *hesed,* we respond by walking in humility, mercy, and justice to fulfill our part in this covenantal love.

Although I feel it is critical to have a Core Affirmation with "because God" first and "we respond" second, I do not feel it is critical for the sermon to be shaped in this order. Some sermon forms look at God first, some start with the human condition; some bookend the sermon with God, others place God in the middle. All of these forms have the potential for success. However, approaching any sermon form with a Core Affirmation in mind that prioritizes God's action can help ensure the Good News of God's work in and among us is the beacon shining most brightly in your proclamation.

Conclusion

Preaching justice is not about learning a new kind of sermon template. It's about recognizing the gospel's pervasive call to move from self-centered individualism toward neighbor-loving communion. It's about learning to extend ourselves more mercifully as we walk more humbly, embracing a spirit of courageous vulnerability as we share the journey with our communities. Such a justice-minded journey is enabled through communion with our innately relational God, which will ultimately transform our entire understanding of the meaning of "relationship."

We are far more accustomed to the kinds of relationships that operate out of contractual obligation. What must I do to earn or keep the love and respect of another? How can my church operate in a way that attracts people and funds budgets?

Our instincts are often aligned with the Israel we meet in Micah 6—what must we bring to the table in order to have the life we desire?

This contractual understanding of relationship must necessarily be structured by rules and regulations, which lends itself to the most pejorative approach to preaching—the kind that suggests a petty, punishing God more concerned with our failures than with our earnest, if flawed, efforts. Alternatively, when we understand that our relationship with God is rooted in *hesed*, in mutual delight, in the opportunity to be a vibrant, diverse, flourishing community of faith and love and justice, then we have the freedom to be curious seekers of truth—in the gray areas, at the margins, deep within the painful places of conflict and challenge we would prefer to avoid. This is where the God of justice meets us. This is where we learn to embody the Good News of God's promises.

SERMON | Sacred Allyship | Exodus 2:5–10

Rev. Brenda Bertrand
(Fuller Seminary Chaplain)
Fuller Seminary Chapel—February 2, 2022
Available via Podcast or on YouTube[10]

> The daughter of Pharaoh came down to bathe at the river, while her attendants walked beside the river. She saw the basket among the reeds and sent her maid to bring it. When she opened it, she saw the child. He was crying, and she took pity on him. "This must be one of the Hebrews' children," she said. Then

> his sister said to Pharaoh's daughter, "Shall I go and
> get you a nurse from the Hebrew women to nurse
> the child for you?" Pharaoh's daughter said to her,
> "Yes." So the girl went and called the child's mother.
> Pharaoh's daughter said to her, "Take this child and
> nurse it for me, and I will give you your wages." So
> the woman took the child and nursed it. When the
> child grew up, she brought him to Pharaoh's daughter,
> and he became her son. She named him Moses,
> "because," she said, "I drew him out of the water."
> — EXODUS 2:5–10

In the 2021–2022 school year, the All-Seminary Chapel theme at Fuller was "People of God and the Community of Faith," which was explored particularly through sermons that lifted up frequently unseen or forgotten women of the Old Testament. For an entire year, the gospel was proclaimed through the testimonies of Eve, Sarah, Hagar, Deborah, Miriam, Rachel and Leah, Job's wife, the Hebrew midwives, and so many more. In this particular service, we reflected on the importance of walking with these women through "A Litany to Honor Women" from *Common Prayer: A Liturgy for Ordinary Radicals*:[11]

> We walk in the company of the women who have gone
> before, mothers of the faith both named and unnamed,
> testifying with ferocity and faith to the Spirit of wisdom
> and healing.

> They are the judges, the prophets, the martyrs, the war-
> riors, poets, lovers and saints who are near to us in the

shadow of awareness, in the crevices of memory, in the
landscape of our dreams. . . .

We walk in the company of you mothers of the faith,
who teach us to resist evil with boldness, to lead with
wisdom, and to heal. Amen.

Rev. Brenda Bertrand stepped into this walk by guiding us on a
journey along the Nile with Jochebed, Miriam, and the North
African Princess. This story is more often recounted as the origin story of Moses. Of course, it is. Moses is the only named
character. We know Jochebed only as Moses' mother, Miriam
as Moses' sister, the princess as Pharaoh's daughter and Moses'
adoptive mother. Brenda does not ignore or diminish the significance of Moses and his origin, but rather demonstrates the
profound contributions of these women who stand just outside
the hero's spotlight. For a hero's story is never his story alone,
and in this case, a brave band of heroines are truly the leading
characters.

*Let's be honest. Without these women, there may be no
Moses. And with these women, Pharaoh's power is thwarted
at every turn. These women are ba-a-a-d.*

*Pharaoh truly prophesied his own demise when he said,
"Kill the boys, but let the girls live," because the women in
this text take him up on his offer, and they come alive in
bold, courageous, creative, and prophetic ways. This is one
of those few biblical texts where every "hero" in the story is
in fact, a heroine.*

We are invited to hear this story in a new way. The action sequences in a film of this story would not depict men in battle, executing dramatic rescues of Hebrew boys, but rather the cunning of the Hebrew women and their allies within the palace. "Kill the boys" is a tragic injustice, to be sure, but "Let the girls live" is the crux of the story. "Let the girls live" is the beginning of what will one day become the Good News of Israel's deliverance out of slavery in Egypt and subsequent journey to the Promised Land.

Although God's name is not mentioned, the Spirit lives large in the subtext. Every woman in this story is guided, transformed, and convicted to do justice. A hero story is about a protagonist's success in opposition to a conflict: man vs. man, man vs. self, man vs. nature, man vs. society. Brenda has already changed this script by making it a woman vs. man story, but she can't stop there because this is not a women's empowerment speech. This is a proclamation of the Good News of the gospel of justice, and the Good News here is that mere humans are not in charge of the story at all. The women behave heroically, they have great success in their roles as protagonists, but their victory is God's victory. Their heroism is the result of the movement of the Spirit in and among them. It is only through the work of the Spirit in us that justice can be done. It is never ours to do alone.

So, let's go to them, in the beautiful land of Egypt, along the banks of the Nile. I want you to push away those tall papyrus reeds and cattails. I want you to imagine the morning sun is bright and it glints off bloody water. We are about to witness a phenomenon: the privileged and the marginalized: connecting, collaborating, and co-leading.

Brenda isn't going to simply tell us about this story; she is going to help us live it. She takes great care in her artful narration to ensure we are immersed in this world, poised to make our own discoveries, even as she directs our attention toward something we may not have watched for before—the act of justice in the privileged and marginalized joining together in Spirit-filled community.

> *In verse five, the princess is on her way to bathe. Can you see her strolling in her morning splendor? She is wealthy, child-free, possibly unmarried. She may take the throne if/ when her father and brothers die—or by some other way, as history suggests. She is privileged, and the system protects her. And for this, she doesn't need a guilt trip or a power trip; she needs allyship. She probably needs friendship, but she needs an opportunity to learn and unlearn how to connect with her own humanity and the humanity of others.*

We are asked not only to lay eyes on the princess, but to see into the depth of her character—an archetype for all those who stroll through their mornings with the assurance of safety and security that privilege provides. As I see the princess in this way, I see myself. I feel that very familiar and thoroughly unhelpful instinct of white guilt begin to rise in me, until Brenda names it. In seeing the princess, she knows her. In seeing the princess, she knows me. She plants these seeds of knowing in a new way.

> *There's an enslaved girl on the scene as well. Can you see her? She's crouching in the reeds, and she's been sent by her mother with a life-altering mission. Hide. Watch your*

brother. Get home safe, and report. If you're seen, don't speak a word. Serve. Play small. Feel the room. Know your place. Know your language. Learn their language. Be your parents' translator. Understand the rules—code switch when you need to. And please, get home safe. Just like the princess, Miriam knows her place. It is hard being seen as a problem, to operate in a system built against you. But Miriam doesn't need saving; she doesn't need pity. She needs an ally, an advocate.

As an African American, Brenda's cultural context helps her understand Miriam's place in the story in a way that my own context cannot. This also happens to be a sermon at the start of Black History Month, and in this brief paragraph, she has told us a great deal about the legacy of the Black experience. I imagine that listeners all too familiar with societal rules that require constant code switching felt seen and understood as Brenda brought our attention to the full depth of Miriam's experience—just as she had done previously with the princess.

And so, privilege and poverty meet. And we need to remember, privilege is a delusion with its own bondage. And marginalization is bondage, and it is oppression. These women are different, but they're both unfree. It is radical to see us all as suffering and unfree, even in our varying degrees of powerlessness and powerfulness.

We are all, regardless of our place in the story, captive to injustice. Brenda was able to bring us to this understanding because of how deeply she has mined the text for truth. Miriam and the princess represent different kinds of truth, but one is not greater than another. It is far too easy in so-called "justice sermons" to pit good people against bad people, to declare that there is only one way to see or to behave, but the truth is never that straightforward. Brenda has brought into the open the complexities of this story, and of our own experience, and in so doing has become an ally to the Word of God and to its work in our lives today.

To be a sacred ally, we must pay attention. There are so many ways in which Brenda's retelling of this story has helped us pay attention. This is the preacher's role—to point out what may be rustling in the reeds, but then to step aside and allow the listeners to look for themselves and identify what's there. *Friends, start looking where you bathe. In your heart, in your home, in staff and faculty meetings, in the classroom, at church, in our neighborhoods, at family dinner. What unfreedom lies awake there that seeks our attention?*

From here, Brenda continues to weave together scripture's story with principles of allyship. When the princess discovers the baby and feels pity, she could easily have become stuck in that pity, maintaining the distance that privilege affords. Instead, *the princess goes from feeling bad for him, to feeling bad with him, and she comes alive. . . . She doesn't have to be Hebrew to feel human depravity.* Allyship is about sharing in one another's suffering, connecting with one another's humanity.

The princess's liberation is part of the Spirit's larger liberative work that's already happening in the baby's family, and the future exodus of an entire nation will be unleashed in her liberation. Authentically connecting with the humanity right in front of her eventually impacts the whole system, and this is a work that has been started long before her and will continue long after her. This is Good News! The princess has chosen to participate in the gospel's promise of liberation. She makes this choice *not from guilt, or fragility, or messiah complex—but from love.*

But the princess is not the only ally at work here. Miriam's attentive listening leads her to respond in courageous creativity because she discerns the *Egyptian princess is worthy of trust, even in a system that has proven unworthy.* These two women will now act out of mutual trust, demonstrating another key aspect of sacred allyship: *that solutions come from within communities, from the oppressed themselves. . . . An ally who sees power beyond their own as equally valid has truly been liberated for the work of justice.* And now two allies become three, as Jochebed is brought into the circle of trust, providing the solution that will not only save Moses, and eventually the Hebrew people, but that will also bring healing to this Hebrew family.

> *Friends, I could barely keep a dry eye when I envisioned this birth mama reunited with her boy. Just hours prior, she's probably rocking on the floor in a corner of her home, faith-filled and grief-stricken all at once. Unable to eat. Unable to speak. Heart completely broken. Tremoring with her post-partum adrenaline. Her body still recovering from a traumatic birth that she couldn't even prove. And then a knock comes on the door. My God. A knock comes on the door all because a privileged daughter and a marginalized one decided to come alive together.*

Brenda has made herself a sacred ally with these women in scripture. She is paying attention. She is connecting with them authentically. She is looking for the solution within their own community—within the canon of scripture. In being a sacred ally to scripture, she has helped us see God's truth in a new way. She has helped us see that the simple (though far from easy) acts of paying attention, of sharing in one another's humanity, and of collaborating in trust enable us to join in the justice of God at work in us, through the power of the Holy Spirit, and according to the liberating work of Christ.

What Christ came to do as the most sacred of allies was to take on flesh and become one of us. Becoming human just like us. And because he lives, so can we. Friends, no matter your ethnic background, gender, socio-economic background, you are worthy of this sacred allyship. To be a receiver and a giver of this holy companioning. Of having someone stand with you and beside you, whether they look like you or not.

By saving this gospel turn for the culmination of the sermon, Brenda has allowed the Old Testament text to speak for itself. She ensured that we saw what was floating in the reeds of the Hebrew experience without forcing it through our New Testament lens. This set forth another kind of gospel truth. The sacred allyship demonstrated by the Egyptian Princess, Miriam, and Jochebed was an expression of God's covenant of *hesed*. This covenant is the foundation of the Good News for us today, and we have the added benefit of living it in the way that Christ has set us free to live.

The next time we see baby Moses, he is a toddler, speaking his mother's tongue—nurtured between two strong women

who resist systems. Who could have imagined this outcome?
Who could have made this up? And we cannot know what
God wants to do through our risks either. Because when we
live, others live. When the girls live, everyone lives.

This sermon was its own kind of risk. It relied on Brenda's attentive discernment to where God was asking her to look and where the Spirit was inviting her to place her trust. Like Miriam, she responded in courageous creativity, extending herself as a sacred ally of story and scripture. She could not know what God wanted to do with the risks she took in this sermon, but this did not stop her from preaching justice by coming alive in this moment of proclamation and modeling with her own actions, "when the girls live, everyone lives."

CHAPTER 3

A Prophetic Witness

When Creator Sets Free (Jesus) saw this great crowd,
he went back up to the mountainside
and down to teach the people.
His followers came to him there, so he took
a deep breath, opened his mouth,
and began to share his wisdom with them and
teach them how to see Creator's good road.

Creator's blessing rests on the poor,
the ones with broken spirits.
The good road from above is theirs to walk.
Creator's blessing rests on the ones
who walk a trail of tears,
for he will wipe the tears from their
eyes and comfort them.
Creator's blessing rests on the ones who
walk softly and in a humble manner.

The earth, land, and sky will welcome
them and always be their home.
Creator's blessing rests on the ones who hunger
and thirst for wrongs to be made right again.
They will eat and drink until they are full.
Creator's blessing rests on the ones who
are merciful and kind to others.
Their kindness will find its way
back to them—full circle.
Creator's blessing rests on the pure of heart.
They are the ones who will see the Great Spirit.
Creator's blessing rests on the ones who make peace.
It will be said of them, "They are the
children of the Great Spirit!"
Creator's blessing rests on the ones
who are hunted down
and mistreated for doing what is right,
for they are walking the good road from above.

Others will lie about you, speak against you, and
look down on you with scorn and contempt,
all because you walk the road with me. This is a
sign that Creator's blessing is resting on you.
So let your hearts be glad and jump for joy, for
you will be honored in the spirit-world above.
You are like the prophets of old, who were
treated in the same way by your ancestors.
— MATTHEW 5:2–12 (FIRST NATIONS VERSION)

The Beatitudes appear in the lectionary on the Fourth Sunday after Epiphany every three years. The season of Epiphany—beginning after the Twelve Days of Christmas and continuing until Ash Wednesday—is our time to look more closely at Jesus's inbreaking into the world. We open our eyes to what the revelation of Christ means for us today.

It makes perfect sense to me that the Beatitudes, as well as subsequent portions of the Sermon on the Mount, are assigned during this season because in Jesus's signature sermon, he is calling an oppressed people to see in a new way. It is a prophetic vision that offers comfort to the afflicted and affliction to the comfortable.

I fear that when we read the Beatitudes today, however, they have lost their sting. We hear only comfort. We hear only: "I'm blessed when I feel poor in spirit; I'm blessed when I feel mournful; I'm blessed when things don't go my way and I'm feeling persecuted." These things are true, but my *feelings* or your *feelings* on any particular day are not what Jesus is talking about here. He is proclaiming an earth-shattering, cosmic reordering of power that will usher in a New Kingdom. The Kingdom of God's economy of mercy, love, and justice will triumph over the empire's economy of narcissism and power mongering, and we need to be on the right side of this culture clash. We've stitched these blessings onto pillows and wall hangings, but they are actually thorns in our flesh.

For Jesus's sermon to be a prophetic call to us today, we need to hear it in a new way. *The First Nations Version* helps us do that. It disrupts what we think we already know about this text, and thereby invites us to see it differently. The language may be unusual, even uncomfortable, to non-Native ears, but it is rooted in the earth around us, from a people who have been worshiping the same God that we know for a very, very long time.

A group of Native church leaders from twenty-five tribes throughout North America partnered with OneBook and

Wycliffe Associates to offer this translation "as our gift to all English-speaking First Nations people and to the entire sacred family, which is the body of the Chosen One." This is a prophetic gift. A gift that restores the privilege of language to a people who have much to teach us about what it is to live as "ones who walk the trail of tears." The dedication page in *The First Nation Version* makes this clear:

> This translation of the good story is dedicated to the Indigenous Peoples of Turtle Island (North America)—the Tribal Nations that call this land home. We pray the First Nations Version will bring healing to those who have suffered under the dominance of colonial governments who, with the help of churches and missionary organizations, often took our land, our languages, our cultures, and even our children. As our Tribal Nations work hard to reclaim what has been stolen, it is our hope that the colonial language that was forced upon us can now serve our people in a good way, by presenting Creator Sets Free (Jesus) in a more culturally relevant context.[1]

In the First Nations context, the Kingdom of Heaven is understood as Creator's Good Road. The concept of the Kingdom of Heaven is of vital importance because it is at the heart of all Jesus's teachings throughout the Gospel of Matthew. Jesus basically has one sermon: "The Kingdom of Heaven is at hand." The Kingdom of Heaven has broken in and is trying to work in the midst of all of us. These Native believers and biblical scholars are helping us understand Kingdom in a profound way. Living as citizens of the Kingdom of Heaven is about journeying together along Creator's Good Road.

Creator's Good Road is a very helpful metaphor because it demonstrates that the Kingdom of Heaven is not some far-off place that we hope we will visit one day after we die. Quite the contrary, it is the road we are walking right now. The Kingdom is here in our midst. It is part of our living, breathing, embodied existence as we put one foot in front of the other right here on the earth.

Jesus knows better than anyone how difficult it is to walk Creator's Good Road, and so his sermon begins with a proclamation of the Good News. Jesus offers the Beatitudes as a matter of fact. Grammatically speaking, they are in the indicative tense. These blessings already exist and are at work all around us. It's not a question of if or when. It's a statement. This is the greatest news for all of us. This is an assurance that as we walk Creator's Good Road, we walk with Jesus, who has these blessings at hand.

On that mountaintop, Jesus was preaching to a gathered crowd of mostly Jewish people who were living under the rule of the Roman government. They were marginalized. They were cast aside. They were not valued. They were less than second-class citizens. Jesus was not talking to them merely about their everyday woes and concerns. He was saying, "This situation you find yourselves in, where you have no power, where you are at the mercy of a cruel government that doesn't understand, that doesn't treat you fairly, this will all change in the coming Kingdom. It will change as you walk with me along Creator's Good Road. Even as you live every single day under the boot of that oppression, you are not alone. I am walking with you."

Jesus was speaking into a context of oppression, and his words continue to speak into such a context today. This is the prophetic cry of his sermon that rings true throughout the ages—oppression in our world, at any time and in any place and toward any people, will not be the last word. It is not the road that God has set before us. It is, however, the road that humanity continually chooses to walk. And the truth is, many of us listening to Jesus's sermon today have more in common with the citizens of Rome than with the Jews who were gathered at that mountain.

What is the Good News, then, for those of us on the side of privilege? For those of us who know little about walking a trail of tears or of being hunted down and mistreated? Do we still get these blessings if we, whether knowingly or unknowingly, are on the oppressors' side of an unjust system? The answer is yes. This message is for all of us, but we must recognize our role in it. We do that by learning from others. Each of us will see more clearly when our eyes are opened by those who receive Jesus's message in a different way.

First Nations people know better than anyone what it means to walk a trail of tears. That is a life experience that I cannot understand, but when I learn through the wisdom and experience of my Native brothers and sisters that Jesus's message is about walking this trail together, and that they are committed to walking with me despite my ignorance or complicity in a history of injustice, it changes the way I see. It changes the way I walk.

To receive the fullness of the Good News Jesus offers here, we must commit to walking Creator's Good Road as a united community, as the Body of Christ. The Beatitudes are then a guide to lead us along that Road. The first step is to walk softly and in a humble manner, which allows us to see and hear more of what's happening around us, to experience the welcome of the earth, land, and sky, as well as our fellow walkers on the road. When I walk in this way, I begin to see what's happening on a part of the road that maybe isn't usually mine to walk.

As I get better at walking softly and humbly, wrongs that need to be made right become more evident, and I begin to hunger and thirst for righteousness.

My hunger and thirst lead me to be more merciful and kind to others, and I am nurtured by receiving kindness in return.

Leaning into this circle of mercy, kindness, and love begins to purify my heart, which allows me to know the Great Spirit, the God who has created and loved me more and more intimately.

Drawing near to the Creator in this way enables me to be one who makes peace. The more I live as a person of peace, the more others recognize the work of the Great Spirit in me.

As we walk farther down this road of blessings, it is very possible that we will be mistreated for doing what is right. Many along this road are all too familiar with the mistreatment of marginalization due to skin color, gender, immigration status, economic means, or any other measure of privilege. Many people have no choice in whether or not to walk this part of the road, and yet their ongoing witness is one of joy in walking with Creator's blessing.

Others of us have the privilege to choose whether we will continue along Creator's Good Road. If we choose to care for a neighbor instead of tending to our own needs first, that will probably influence our bottom line. It might make our lives more difficult in the moment. If we choose to share our power with someone who doesn't have it, that might make our road more challenging. These choices might lead us to feel mistreated. This is not persecution. It does, however, present challenges that influence our choices, making it far too easy to leave the peace-making to someone else, to reserve our mercy and kindness for our inner circle, to hunger and thirst for our own path to be made straight, and thereby cease to walk humbly with all those who call the earth their home.

We have been blessed with all we need to walk Creator's Good Road, but we miss those blessings when we are focused on protecting our own wealth, power, security, or comfort and end up separated from those who are walking softly, humbly, kindly, and thirsting for wrongs to be made right. Jesus's sermon is a prophetic exclamation that the path of the empire is a road to ruin, while Creator's Good Road is a journey to freedom.

My heart leaps for joy that Christ has gone before us on this road and continually reaches out to us, beckoning, "Walk the road with me." May we choose to accept this invitation to journey with soft feet and humble spirits, learning from one another as we open our eyes and ears to the prophetic way of Jesus.

The Preacher as Prophet

I became a preacher quite begrudgingly. Not for what I imagine are the usual reasons, though. I'm not afraid to speak in front of people. I had a former career as a singer and musical theater performer. I'm plenty happy to step into the spotlight, so to speak. I'm an extrovert. I think quickly on my feet. I've got no problem keeping a conversation going. All these things would make it seem, I suppose, that I would be a natural preacher and perhaps even longing to be in the pulpit. That was never the case.

Performing on a stage is one thing. Preaching from a pulpit is something entirely different. The weight and burden of being a voice for God, the burden of giving voice to the gospel, is one I never wanted to bear. It's a weight that I still carry somewhat heavily every time I stand to preach. I've come to understand that it is a gift and a privilege to preach, and I do so now with a significant amount of joy, but it will never not be a burden.

The rub for me is primarily in the prophetic sense of preaching. Must every preacher be sage, priest, *and* prophet? I take some issue with each of those archetypes, actually. A preacher as sage should not mean resident expert with all the answers, but rather a wise asker of questions and facilitator of conversation. A preacher as priest does not have some magical clergy powers or direct hotline to God that isn't also available to each of our listeners, but we do hold the lives of our people in a pastoral way that helps us experience the Word through their joys and challenges. What, then, does it look like to be a preacher as prophet?

I don't believe every preacher is called to be "a prophet" in the same sense as Elijah or Elisha, Micah or Malachi. Some certainly are, and I have been deeply impacted by prophets in my own life who seem to hear the voice of God as a clarion call, carrying the authority of that voice into their message—whether from the pulpit, at the watercooler, or across the kitchen table. God does not speak to me that way, or at least I do not hear God in that way, but I recognize the authenticity of the message as it is spoken through these contemporary prophets I know as friends and partners in ministry.

Biblical prophets spoke truth to power, confronted idolatrous practices, and declared the work of God to be a work of justice in which we must participate. Many of their sermons were confrontational: *"I hate, I despise your religious festivals; your assemblies are a stench to me,"* says the Lord through Amos (5:21–24). *"How the faithful city has become a whore! She that was full of justice, righteousness lodged in her—but now murderers!"* declares the Lord through Isaiah (1:21).

As preachers today become more convinced of the need to speak truth to power as an act of justice, these types of prophetic confrontations may be most on our mind. But this would not be true to the full voice of the prophets in scripture. A significant portion of prophetic proclamation is Good News. *"Rejoice and exult with all your heart, O daughter Jerusalem!"* declares Zephaniah, *"The Lord has taken away the judgments against you, he has turned away your enemies"* (3:14–15). Pastoral comfort and hope are delivered through prophets such as Jeremiah, offering the Lord's assurance, *"For I know the plans I have for you, plans to prosper you and not to harm you"* (29:11). Biblical prophets were also sage-like. In 2 Samuel 12, for example, Nathan's parable of the poor man's lamb wisely leads David to recognize his iniquity. And they were priestly— Jeremiah weeps for Jerusalem, Daniel is a prayer warrior on behalf of Israel, Moses returns to the Lord again and again to advocate for the people.

All of this leads me to wonder if the role of preacher as prophet, for most of us, is more akin to the role of witness. We are witnesses who disrupt the complacency that makes us fail to smell the stench of our idolatry and unrighteousness, as well as the complacency that makes us fail to rejoice in the provision and deliverance of a God who loves us.

The Prophet as Witness

In Thomas Long's book *The Witness of Preaching*, he explains, "The verb 'to witness' has two main meanings: to see and to tell." To be a witness, you must first "behold" something; you must be "present and active as an observer." You must "take something in." But it doesn't stop there, because a witness also has to "give something out." What they *saw* they now have to *say*. What they *perceived*, they will *testify*.[2]

Every biblical prophet receives a specific message from God and then speaks it to the people. From Moses to Isaiah to Jesus it's always the same—they see and they tell. You could say that the role of the sage is also a witness—to learn and then teach. Even the role of a priest is a witness—to take in the experience of the people and then share God's presence in that experience. The role of prophet as witness carries a more peculiar burden, though. The prophet beholds a message directly from God that is meant specifically for *their* people, the particular community to whom God has called them to speak.

The call to preach bears the responsibility of being a faithful witness, seeking the truth that may disrupt what we thought we already knew. We go to the text on behalf of the people, praying that we might behold a message from God, and then we have to testify. This sounds to me an awful lot like the work of a prophet.

To preach as a prophet is to embody the Word as it lives and breathes among God's people now, drawing us into a community of faith that began in the distant past, and pointing us toward an eschatological future rooted in the incarnation, crucifixion, and resurrection of Jesus Christ. This is a prophetic witness.

As prophetic witnesses, each of us is asked to speak the truth as it appears uniquely to us, as we hold in our hearts the needs of a particular community. What is the truth *I* perceive God to be speaking in scripture and in the world, and that most needs to be heard at this time, among these people? Each of us sees truth in a different way, but collectively—and only collectively—the fullness of God's truth can be revealed. We need the disruption of having to refocus our lens to see what that witness over *there* sees, so that we end up seeing what is going on right *here* more truthfully. That's why it takes a multitude of voices to fulfill this call to preaching, and that's why I believe preachers are called to be part of a prophetic community. One preacher cannot seek to speak for all. We are all walking Creator's Good Road together, which allows us the gift of seeing and hearing through a diversity of voices, revealing how God's grace and presence are moving among us in extraordinary ways.

Ultimately, this is how the preacher as prophet is equipped to preach the gospel of justice. We open ourselves to continually *receive* the witness of others so that we can more faithfully, more prophetically, *be* a witness to others. This means confronting our own relationships with power and privilege. It means learning to stand inside pain, rather than walling ourselves off from it. It means learning to discern the Good News of Christ's redeeming work in the world in the most unexpected places.

The Prophetic Witness Is Imaginative

In 2022, twenty or so Micah Group leaders gathered for several days to discern together how we might reshape this movement of empowered, wise preachers who are committed to doing justice into a movement that would nurture a prophetic community for preachers. On one level, this does not seem like a major shift to us. Our goal is still to support empowered, wise, justice-seeking preaching, but we believe the way to do that is through commitment to our own formation within a prophetic community. This is a commitment to receive the witness of others—especially others who are very different from ourselves, whether in gender, ethnicity, denomination, age, or socio-economic contexts—in order to disrupt our own patterns of complacency.

One thing that became abundantly clear in our discussions was that the prophetic community we were envisioning might be *for* preachers, but it could not be made up solely *of* preachers. We needed opportunities for discernment around encounters with cross-vocational voices to stir our imaginations beyond the boundaries of our own experience. Artists, business leaders, activists, and politicians could all provide vital new understanding, stoking our collective prophetic imagination.

In Walter Brueggemann's seminal book *The Prophetic Imagination*, he argues that the Christian tradition, "having been co-opted by the king," has fallen into a collective state of "numbness," tending toward the false smiles and insincere platitudes of "crossless good news and a future well-being without a present anguish." The prophetic imagination has the power "to cut through the numbness, to penetrate the self-deception, so that the God of endings is confessed as Lord."[3] The God of endings does not deny the stench of death, but has conquered it. The prophetic ministry of Jesus did not gloss over human pain and suffering, but endured it. The power of the Holy Spirit does not remove the fear of terror or injustice, but comforts us within it. Siloed preaching that fails to take note of the disruptive witness from culture—the lament of artists, the fear in the marketplace, the anger of politics—will fail to cut through the numbness. It will fail to preach the gospel of justice. It will fail to proclaim truly Good News.

It is not enough for worship and preaching to stimulate the intellect; it must also stimulate the imagination. The language of biblical prophets is rich in metaphor and storytelling— Ezekiel's dry bones, Isaiah's potter with clay, the countless parables of Jesus, to name just a few. Even Paul, perhaps the most classically expository preacher in the Bible, gives us the body with many members, running the good race, and a building with Christ as the cornerstone.

Stimulating the imagination through language and storytelling is not a particularly new idea, and I suppose it is the instinct that leads some preachers to use aesthetic or cultural offerings as sermon illustrations. Indeed, many a preaching workshop is built around how to find new sermon illustrations, and the advice given often has to do with engaging more forms of art—literature, poetry, paintings, sculpture, film, and music—and to use more media and technology in sermons and worship. This is good advice, to a certain extent. Learning to navigate the pros and cons of cultural, industrial, or scientific advances in any age has been, and will continue to be, a growing edge for any preacher. Expanding one's own horizons through art, media, and technology will surely aid in that growth. However, turning to art and culture for the express purpose of illustrating a sermon or enhancing a worship experience limits its potential for revelation by attempting to force a particular meaning on a given creative expression. It limits the opportunity for art, or for artists, to be a prophetic voice.

Listening to a song, watching a film clip, or offering a piece of art solely to bolster an idea the preacher has already expressed actually robs art of its true purpose, which is to point to something beyond itself. Using art as illustration, then, is little more than propaganda, meant simply to give visual reinforcement to intellectual thought far too often entrenched in complacency and numbness. Instead, for art to speak most effectively, it must be allowed to disrupt. It must be given space for imaginative revelation.

We should absolutely use art and literature and music and film in both our preparation to preach and the preaching itself, but do so in ways that offer freedom of thought and open up the possibility of more questions rather than definitive answers. We do so in a way that stimulates a prophetic imagination for truth in the undefined, for sacred in the profane. Preachers who are nurtured through a prophetic community that includes artists, thinkers, and leaders not only from within the church but also from popular culture and the public square are preachers whose growing imagination may reveal a path less traveled along Creator's Good Road.

The Prophetic Imagination Is Curious, Creative, and Courageous

Much of my work with preachers at Fuller Seminary is situated with the Brehm Center, which is dedicated to integrating worship, theology, and the arts for the renewal of church and culture.[4] As a musician myself, my own approach to preaching is very much aligned with this integration, and I began to wonder if engagement with the arts might help other preachers as well—especially those with no self-described artistic abilities. What is it about the way artists move in the world that impacts our ability to witness in unique ways?

The product that an artist creates may be the medium through which they "testify," but the way in which they "see" has much more to do with the process than with the product. Whatever the discipline—visual art, music, dance, photography, filmmaking, culinary arts, poetry, literature—an artist must learn certain fundamental practices of "making," which they continually rehearse, refine, build upon, and fight against. As they do so, they learn how to see, how to hear, how to taste, how to feel, and eventually how to express all of that seeing and feeling into what we call art. For some, this process is mainly about learning a technique. For me, it is a spiritual discipline.

Through the process of experimenting with, and especially struggling with, rudimentary art-making practices, we have the opportunity to engage in a form of embodied spiritual contemplation that facilitates an imaginative space for embracing the invitation to be co-creators with God. You do not have to be an artist to accept this invitation! Anyone can learn to see and hear and feel in new ways by simply submitting to a repeated creative practice that expands the imagination. More specifically, when preachers submit to such a practice, it has the potential to stimulate a prophetic ministry of creativity, curiosity, and courage (3Cs).[5]

I have come to believe that these 3Cs are vital to a flourishing ministry at the convergence of worship, preaching, and justice where the prophetic call to preachers requires *curiosity* toward what God is already doing in their community, *creativity* to engage new approaches to living that mission through a life of worship inside and outside the sanctuary, and *courage* to proclaim this disruptive, prophetic witness from the pulpit.

Curiosity

An instinct of curiosity inspires people in power to ask more questions and issue fewer dictums. Probing more deeply into the anxieties and hopes of a community, for example, can open new avenues of dialogue and influence the manner in which decisions are made, not to mention the nature of the decisions themselves. This is itself an act of justice, as it is an opportunity to redistribute power away from a privileged few and into the hands of the full community.

Furthermore, curiosity engages a sense of empathy that aids in moving people through the discomfort of change. This sense of curious empathy is especially critical in the work of justice, where conflict often leads to polarizing ideologies that attempt to simplify one another's narratives through assumption and stereotyping rather than wading into the deeper complexities of the issue. Empathetic curiosity leads not only to asking more questions, but also to asking better questions:

What is a personal experience that may be impacting your feelings about this?
What is most mystifying to you about people who hold this view?
What would you like to know about them? What do you want them to know about you?[6]

Preaching from this place of empathetic curiosity can particularly help to expose biases within a church community and begin to remove barriers that prevent shared visioning and decision-making in a church's collective witness.

Creativity
God has called us to be agents of a changing world, a yet-unforeseen new creation, and yet we are not the ones responsible for the final reality. Creativity, then, must be understood as a joint effort between God and God's people in which we are to be more concerned with the journey than the destination. This means making space, giving time, and fostering an environment of learning, failure, and practice. Embracing creativity is not about producing something new or beautiful but about immersing yourself in a process of allowing curiosity to lead into exploration.

As a preacher grows in their personal expression of creativity, their imagination will likely become more and more generative. This may begin from the essentially narcissistic place of experiencing God through a very personal creative lens, but the more our creativity grows, the more we become aware of the dominant symbols and metaphors emanating from our own aesthetic preferences. From here, a church leader is better equipped to critically assess the dominant symbols and metaphors within their worship space.

Does the imagery used in bulletin covers, worship slides, banners, and church websites reflect a vibrant imagination for the past, present, and future of God's Kingdom?

Do the hymns, praise songs, and other musical offerings not merely reflect the taste or preference of dominant voices in the community but also draw worshipers into the history of our faith and the future of a mission both local and global?

Do sermon illustrations and references reflect a broad range of voices and interests rather than tending toward particular affinities?

Moving toward an emphatic "yes" to each of these questions is a big step toward creative leadership that is rooted in the gospel of justice.

Courage

Courage is, arguably, an important characteristic for any type of leader, but it is particularly vital to a preacher seeking to be a prophetic witness. It is one thing to develop one's own ability to see and sit with uncomfortable truth, but it is quite another to give voice to it and to call others to see and sit with it. Strengthening muscles of curiosity and creativity helps foster courage to step outside our comfort zones and engage with others as an exercise of vulnerability.

The church is meant to be an institution where this type of courageous, curious, creative engagement is an ongoing part of formation and discipleship, but all too often, churches (and perhaps especially church leadership) are more invested in promoting their communities as "safe" or "peaceful" or an "escape" from the affront of the outside world. This is the trap of numbness called out by Brueggemann. It takes courage to facilitate a disruption that stirs up the prophetic imagination of a community more inclined toward stagnant pew-sitting and silencing of critical voices than toward loving God and neighbor according to the gospel of justice.

PRAXIS—Developing the 3Cs

Learning a Creative Practice

Every act of preaching is a creative act. Every single time we go to the Word on behalf of God's people, we are engaging in a creative process that helps us experience anew what God has already done, and what God is continuing to do, in the life of our communities and in the world around us. The preacher's prophetic witness is a creative one.

Some consider preaching an art in itself. I tend to agree, to the extent that it is an act of creating, which is an act of art. Where I differ from some homiletical schools of thought, however, is that I do not consider preaching to be performance art. Performance is involved. There are some of the same mechanics that are important for things like acting and public speaking, but despite the fact that listeners may feel entertained by some sermons, they are not for the purpose of entertainment. When we approach them as such, we end up focusing more on the product than on the process. We treat the art of preaching as a means to illustrate a point or answer a question, rather than allowing it to be a creative, prophetic witness that points beyond itself. This is where engagement with other types of creativity, other types of art, can help us grow those instincts of curiosity, creativity, and courage.

The best way to lean into an artist's approach to these 3Cs is to engage with the artists all around you. This is an opportunity to walk a different part of Creator's Good Road than you may have before. Talk to the artists in your church. Seek out the artists in your community. Go to a jazz club. Sit in a poetry slam. Laugh at an improv night. Pay attention to those voices that stir something in you—whether positively or negatively—and invite them into conversation. Find out how they do what they do, how they see what they see, how they feel what they feel. Learn how their art-making process helps them make sense of the world. Whether the artist is a believer or not, what kind of response might their art make to God? A lament? A protest? An offering of gratitude?

Consider what small, very basic part of their artistic process you might practice yourself. Better yet—ask them to teach you. A musician might create a playlist to help you listen for sounds you haven't noticed before. A poet might suggest a journaling exercise to reshape your use of language. An actor or dancer might demonstrate a series of movements to express ideas or feelings without words.

Remember, this is not about a product, it is about a practice. You are not trying to become the artist they are. You are trying to see the way they see, which will only ever be the way that *you* see, but now you are able to see through a new lens. Your creative practice may lead to a product, and you may even be willing to call it "art," or at least describe it as "artful," but the end result is not the goal. The art itself will not be your eventual sermon illustration, although you will no doubt discover that you have many new illustrations to share. When you embrace this kind of creative quest in your own life, the illustrations that it will bring to your sermons will not be the art that you create but the journey that you had while engaging in prophetic community.

Developing a Spiritual Practice in Creativity
While any level of engagement with art and artists will surely help inspire a preacher's prophetic imagination, I firmly believe it is not enough to be mere consumers or observers of art. We must be makers and creators ourselves—separate from the creation of a sermon. This isn't about becoming a sculptor, pianist, or photographer. It's about paying attention to the places in our lives where we already exercise a form of creativity and allowing it to stir our imaginations. Inventing a new soup recipe, making a garden planter out of an old bucket, or improvising a bedtime story are all opportunities for creative practice.

I've developed an online course, *Artful Leadership*, that is available to anyone wishing to further explore this idea and engage in art-based training to stimulate creativity, curiosity, and courage in church leadership.[7] What it all boils down to, though, is committing to practices of art-making as a matter of spiritual discipline. This type of embodied imagination invites a disruption in our usual patterns of thinking and seeing.

As you grow in relationship with artists in your community, and you learn ways to engage in new artistic practices, consider how you might use that practice as a regularly repeated spiritual discipline. (You will also find suggestions in *Appendix B*). Commit to engaging in this practice every day, or as frequently as possible, for at least a week or two.

The daily repetition is more important than the amount of time spent. Whether you have ten minutes or an hour, returning to the same practice again and again is the best way to build your muscles of creativity, curiosity, and courage. Choose a specific time each day, put it on your calendar, set a daily alarm, and stick to your practice.

Throughout the week or two, jot down reflections to keep track of how your body, mind, and spirit are responding to your practice. Consider things like:

In what ways is the practice easy or difficult to maintain? What feels like a reward, and what is more burdensome?

In what ways is the practice helping you to experience (or fail to experience) the presence of God?

Have other parts of your day been impacted, whether positively or negatively?

Periodically, give yourself a creativity, curiosity, and/or courage score in relation to aspects of your life or leadership you want to see grow. Pay attention to ways in which your practice may be impacting these scores.

If something is not working for you, try experimenting with various adjustments to the practice before giving it up completely. After you've spent a week or more with a particular practice, try adopting a new one—especially one that pushes you outside your comfort zone. Allow the Holy Spirit to move in this discomfort, fighting the numbness that is the enemy of prophetic imagination.

Conclusion

Prophets are witnesses to truth—the truth of humanity's preference for chasing the power of empire rather than the power of grace, and the truth of God's persistent love and mercy that offers the greater freedom. Jesus prophesied to these dual truths in the Sermon on the Mount, demonstrating the Good News of blessings that rest on those who walk Creator's Good Road and are fortified by the alternative power of the Kingdom of God. The preacher's burden is to be a prophetic witness to this gospel of justice, and especially to its particular call to each particular community that is listening to our particular voice.

No matter the size of the congregation, the resources of its budget, or the diversity of its people, God has already provided the blessings needed for each community to live out its particular mission in God's kingdom. This is a call, in one form or another, to do justice by loving God and neighbor more than self and empire. The prophetic witness must be a disruption to the numbness of stagnant pew-sitting that may suggest otherwise. The *First Nations Version* disrupts what we think we understand about the teaching of the New Testament. Artists and the arts disrupt the way we normally see the world. Engaging in the language and rituals of other cultures disrupt the way we experience fellowship with the people of God and with all God's creation.

Disruption is uncomfortable. Our bodies are the first to tell us this, via tense muscles, churning stomachs, or splitting headaches. We protect ourselves by refusing to receive the disruption, pushing it away as something that's wrong and should be silenced lest it create any further discomfort. Preaching as a prophetic witness helps point to the discomfort and, instead of shutting it down, asks "How might God be speaking to us if we keep listening?"

This means the preacher as prophetic witness must begin by investigating their own penchant for shutting down discomfort. Where have we allowed a desire for power or likeability or job security to squash our courage to seek truth? How have we compromised the gospel by failing to receive the witness of "the other" with open curiosity? When have we been too tired or frustrated or angry to allow for creative discovery of the Good News at work all around us?

As each of us walks Creator's Good Road—preachers, listeners, disciples all—we will stumble. In fact, we will fall again and again and again and again. We are like toddlers struggling to stay on our feet as we learn to walk. Would a parent ever chastise a child by insisting, "Stop falling down!"? Certainly not. The only appropriate response is to cheer for the child's efforts and point to the future we know will come. "Look, you're walking! You're walking!"[8]

God cheers for us with all the joy and hopeful anticipation of a loving parent, and the prophetic witness must point to this cheering. The prophetic witness does not ignore the scrapes and bruises of falling. It welcomes them as an opportunity for growth through healing, tends to them lovingly and truthfully, and all the while holds with hope the Good News that we are being formed as a community of walkers along a very Good Road.

SERMON | Through the Unknown | Mark 4:26–29

Dr. Cindy S. Lee
(Spiritual Director;
Doctoral Projects Administrator and Affiliate Assistant Professor at
Fuller Seminary)
Fuller Seminary Chapel—January 25, 2023
Available via Podcast or on YouTube[9]

> He also said, "This is what the kingdom of God is like.
> A man scatters seed on the ground.
> Night and day, whether he sleeps or gets up,
> the seed sprouts and grows,
> though he does not know how.
> All by itself the soil produces grain—
> first the stalk, then the head,
> then the full kernel in the head.
> As soon as the grain is ripe,
> he puts the sickle to it, because the harvest has come."
>
> — MARK 4:26–29

"I'm a bit frazzled today," revealed Chapel Director Julie Tai at the start of worship. Two days earlier, on January 23, 2023, a mass shooting in Half Moon Bay, CA, had killed seven people. And two days before that, on January 21, 2023, eleven people were killed and nine injured in a mass shooting during a Lunar New

Year festival in Monterey Park, CA. The gunmen and majority of the victims in both shootings were of Asian descent. These were not the first mass shooting tragedies of 2023, certainly not the last, and they had taken a particular toll on the Asian American community. "Lunar New Year is a very important holiday for us," Julie explained. "We're supposed to be here with hope, with excitement for the spring that has sprung out of winter. This is an opportunity for blessings and for family to gather, even when we hate each other, to dine around a table like this."

The communion table prepared at the front of the worship space was a round banquet table, the kind you'd more often find in a fellowship hall. Later, the Lord's Supper would be shared around this table, eight people at a time, pouring Japanese tea for one another and sharing steamed buns. The table was itself a prophetic disruption, asking us to experience this sacramental fellowship according to a different tradition, with an unusual bread and cup, but a familiar time of communing together with Christ.

Great care was taken in this time of worship, largely led by Asian Americans, to create space for Asian American kin, but all of us were invited to join in grief and remembrance and hope together. In an invocational prayer, Julie cried out, "We're here grieving, God. Would you be with us? Please? This is a collective trauma we have endured, and a collective healing that we need." She also invited those of us unfamiliar with the Asian traditions that would be part of this service to set aside our own discomfort to make space for this collective mourning and collective healing. "Today is going to be a wonderful, beautiful mess. Because when family gathers, it's a wonderful, beautiful mess. . . . This is how family works. Welcome to the family."

Dr. Cindy Lee further embraced this beautiful mess in her sermon by offering introductory quotes about the nature of heaven according to Confucius, Lao Tsu, and Chuang Tsu as the starting point for a reflection on the nature of wisdom. *In our passage today, Jesus joins a long line of wisdom teachers who talked about a way of life that he called the kingdom of God or the kingdom of heaven.*

This is a disruption right from the start. Cindy intentionally practices Asian American–centered preaching in order to displace the western-centered approaches to worship that are far more prevalent, including in churches made up entirely of Asian immigrants or of Asian Americans. Her goal, in her own words, is that "Asian Americans listening get an embodied experience of what it's like to be centered, and for the white folks listening to practice not being centered."

I have learned from Asian Christians that they are often taught to keep different religious traditions separate. Shamanism, Buddhism, and Confucianism may contribute positively to cultural ideology and practice, but such syncretism is not meant to influence Christian theology. This cultural complexity is unfamiliar to my own context, and yet I, too, feel a certain tension rise in my body when first asked to consider Jesus in line with these other teachers. But I don't want to allow that rub to stop me from listening. Wisdom comes in many forms, from many voices and traditions. Is it not possible to hold the divine wisdom of Jesus as primary, even as we learn from the wisdom of other sacred texts? This seems to be the courageous, disruptive, prophetic path Cindy is walking, and I want to continue walking with her.

What wisdom teachers know is that we can't change peo-
ple through debate and truth claims, but that stories can
somehow form us. In the wisdom tradition, sages don't give
answers. They hold the mysteries, they ask good questions,
and they tell stories. They give us the space to encounter
divine mystery on our own.

Here is the sagely role of a preacher, a role that works in partnership with that of prophetic witness. We may wish that Jesus
chose to teach more plainly and directly, but parables are a deeper
source of wisdom that arise from and instigate prophetic imagination. Cindy's curiosity encouraged her to look more closely at
this particular parable, wondering *What made my brain skip this*
story all these years? She wondered what new way of life this parable might offer as it invites us into a renewed story.

In this story, the farmer's life is dependent on a process that
he doesn't fully know or understand how it works. He is
completely dependent on the grace and mercy of the earth to
provide year after year. The farmer's reality is actually our
reality too, it's just that we fiercely resist this reality. We are
so fiercely independent that we resist the vulnerability of
this dependence. We resist by trying to know everything and
to grow things ourselves.

A prophet defines reality. They help us to see the truth of our
condition. Cindy's prophetic witness is that the truth is that
we depend on processes that we don't fully understand, and yet
we insist that we know best, that human ingenuity can rise to
any challenge, including the challenge of confronting unjust
systems. *You see, historically, we have all been reading the gospels*

and especially the kingdom parables with colonizers' eyes, thinking that the kingdom is something we make happen, through building, through conquest, through winning and controlling others. Ah, now the common reality between this seemingly antiquated story and our life today is becoming plainer. Now we begin to see how this agrarian ode to the Kingdom of God is a part of Jesus's testimony to a gospel of justice.

> *Colonizing is both atrocious acts of injustice and violence towards Indigenous communities, and it is a worldview. A colonizing worldview believes that our natural world is for our own utility and consumption and can be controlled, the colonizing worldview is one we've all bought into in our consuming culture. We have all bought into this worldview in our consuming ways. This worldview has easily led then to the false belief that land and other peoples could be taken and used for our own utility, consumption, and control.*

This is a courageous, prophetic witness to the truth of Christianity's corruption by empire, a truth that lurks at the edges of a numb church, a truth that evidences our utter failure to be a sacred community of neighbor lovers and earth stewards.

> *Our relationship to the earth, then, reveals the conditions of our own hearts. How have you been fiercely gripping to your sense of control? In what ways have we tried to control other people and even God in the same way that we have tried to control the earth? Control and power are our human response to the fears of what we do not know and losing our sense of control.*

The big, bad failure of humanity as a whole, or of the Christian church in particular, is often too much for us to wrap our heads around. We become defensive, "That's not me. I'm not a racist. I have friends of color. I'm not a colonizer." Cindy is a wise prophet and understands this all too well. She does not allow us to become paralyzed by the enormity of this systemic sin but asks us to consider what may be our place in it. How have we adopted the empire's worldview as opposed to that of Jesus? Now we're forced to consider this parable more personally. Do I try to control things? Why yes, yes I do.

In all the kingdom parables the kingdom is not one that comes through building, or conquest or knowledge. Instead, the kingdom is a way of life received as children receive, celebrated like a banquet, valued like finding something we lost, but it is never forced. The kingdom way is a journey, a road we walk, a discipline we practice, an embrace of all the beginnings and endings and everything in between. *We are simply invited into and drawn into this kingdom way, the way of heaven already happening, for all creation already lives heaven's way.* This is the Good News that provides all the blessings we need to fulfill our calling as people of God.

We are not the builders or conquerors or experts. We are sojourners along heaven's way. But this is not to say that we do not have work to do. *If the kingdom is simply to be understood and accepted through truth statements, then we become walking heads. But if the kingdom is experienced, if the kingdom is lived here and now, then we embody the way of Jesus.* As we learn to walk in the way of Jesus, we become co-laborers in the kingdom's economy of love, rather than co-conspirators in the colonizer's economy of conquest.

At the very center of this parable is a healing phrase: we do not know how, we do not know how, we do not know how, and that's okay. This is confession. It is repentance. It is acknowledging our penchant for falling down. We keep trying and getting it wrong. In accepting the vulnerability of not knowing, confessing that we do not know, but scattering our seeds on the ground anyway, we will be blessed with a bounty at harvest time.

> *There is in this parable a beautiful and simple cyclical rhythm found in night and day, sleep and wakefulness. It is a rhythm of watching the earth grow, die, and come to life again. In that rhythm, the earth provides for us and heals us. . . . We were never in control. The earth has always been teaching us our utter dependence, all while we've been futilely striving for our independence. The invitation to dependence is restful. The gospel is not dependent on you, I think that's pretty good news.*

Did you see this rhythm in the parable when you first read it? I did not, and so I am particularly grateful for Cindy's curiosity that led her to this simple, and truly profound, prophetic vision—the earth's consistent rhythm of life, death, and renewal is heaven's way. For all our science and innovation, we cannot fundamentally alter this rhythm, and so true freedom is found in accepting our dependence upon it, our dependence upon the unknown. We grieve and lament the reality of death, the reality of suffering, the reality of injustice, and yet we continue to sow seeds of love and mercy, watching and hoping as they grow and ripen into a new harvest.

This sermon was preached on the fifth day of the Lunar New Year, the marking of another cyclical rhythm based upon the lunar calendar, and this time marked by the mass shooting violence in California. *Collectively, we enter this cycle with fragile and tender hearts. We hold our griefs, trauma, anger, and confusion. But somehow that makes it even more important that we eat together, that we celebrate life together, that we be in community together. It is our act of resistance to the violence.* Celebration as an act of resistance is an act of prophetic imagination. It casts a vision toward the hope of the future's bountiful harvest, despite the seemingly barren fields of the present.

The lunar calendar invites us to look up. See the moon? See how it changes? So do our lives change, too. Just like our parable today, the lunar calendar invites us into a cyclical rhythm of life. Here is another disruption—the disruption of the western understanding of time. *These two calendars are a constant reminder to us that the rhythm of the western calendar, that dominates our economies and has come to represent around the clock production and consumption, is not the only rhythm of life.*

Cindy invites us into the rhythm of heaven's way, where we are not bound by the precision or convention of scientific measurement or technological advancement, but simply dependent upon the mysteries of God. *What's really different about the lunar rhythm is that anyone and everyone can see the moon. We don't need special instruments. It teaches us a spiritual practice to daily observe the cycles of change.* Perhaps we need courage to look up at the moon so we might see a new kind of truth—a truth that is found only when we release our control and allow God's rhythm to permeate our lives.

When the ancient Chinese philosophers saw this cyclical rhythm of night and day, moon and sun, they realized that this rhythm acknowledges our reality. That we live in the cycles of celebration and mourning, pain and joy, good and evil. So in our posture of prayer we learn to hold these realities together. Even if we can't explain it, we can't reason it, even if it feels we don't have control, we keep on holding our prayers. We keep on waking and sleeping. We keep on eating. We keep on depending on another. We keep on depending on God.

Prayer, worship, turning our individual and collective faces toward the glory of God all help us live into the Good News that we are dependent upon God, and one another, and not in control ourselves. Our posture of worship is then the beautiful mess we offer to God in acts of celebration, of lament, of gratitude, and of anguish.

And then on the 15th day of the new year, when the moon is full, round and bright we will gather again. We will celebrate again. This time even bigger, brighter and louder. We gather not just as families but as a city. We will light lanterns. Lanterns everywhere, colorful, beautiful and bright, to scare away the evil that taunts us. We will light lanterns to light our steps forward even through the unknowns. We will eat round, sweet, and sticky things to remember our unity and our dependence on one another. And then we will pray. We will recognize our dependence, and may God have grace and mercy on us all. Amen.

Helping us experience the lunar calendar and the western calendar side-by-side is an example of an instinct that is vital to Cindy's sense of prophetic calling as a preacher. As she described it to me:

I want to challenge the ways in which a western-dominated faith has taught Asians and Asian Americans that our own cultural traditions were "evil." This has caused us an internal disassociation. I believe it takes deep internal and formational work to undo all those internalized messages. Sermons can play a really important role in that work because they are experiential.

Cindy has invited us into a prophetic experience. Her poetic storytelling is a creative offering that has arisen from her willingness to engage scripture with open-handed curiosity and testify to what she beheld. Her prophetic witness as a preacher has invited us into a tactile world of celebration with lights and colors and tastes and smells that give voice to a current anguish and point to a future hope. Her courage to center the Asian American experience has offered a disruption to what we think we know. But we do not know, we do not know, we do not know.

May we, as listeners, have the curiosity to lean into the discomfort of not knowing, receiving disruption as an opportunity to grow our prophetic imagination.

May we, as preachers, have the courage to lean into the discomfort of the disruptions revealed in the complexities of our own experiences, and to boldly testify as prophetic witnesses.

Conclusion

A Life of Worship

> I appeal to you therefore, brothers and sisters, by the
> mercies of God, to present your bodies as a living
> sacrifice, holy and acceptable to God, which is your
> spiritual worship. Do not be conformed to this
> world, but be transformed by the renewing of your
> minds, so that you may discern what is the will of
> God—what is good and acceptable and perfect. For
> by the grace given to me I say to everyone among
> you not to think of yourself more highly than you
> ought to think but to think with sober judgment,
> each according to the measure of faith that God has
> assigned. For as in one body we have many members
> and not all the members have the same function,
> so we, who are many, are one body in Christ, and
> individually we are members one of another.
>
> —ROMANS 12:1–5

The Apostle Paul's appeal to "present your bodies as a living sacrifice" in an act of worship is a call to bring our whole
selves, our whole lives, into communion with God. In so doing,
those very bodies, lives, and minds will be transformed. Such

transformation is the result of a community's spiritual formation as people who do not merely sing and pray about the character of God, but who strive to embody the character of God. We become a community formed by the Good News in order to live the Good News. We become people who live a gospel of justice.

A life of worship is the concluding theme of this book, but it is the beginning, middle, and end of our formation as Good News people. Without worship, the indomitable forces of biology and sociology will have their way; we will be conformed to this world. We will succumb to our inborn, tribal instincts that prioritize safety and power over justice and compassion. As is the case with learning any new skill or habit, it must be practiced. When we gather as a community of worship, we practice being a counter-cultural community that is transformed into the Body of Christ.

Worship Helps Us Live a Call to Community

For Paul, spiritual worship is about orienting our daily thoughts, decisions, and actions toward God. He is not necessarily talking about liturgy or what a corporate body does together in a sanctuary, but he is most definitely talking, once again, about a *plural you* understanding of our lives within the Body of Christ. We have our personal, individual work to do. Each individual mind must be renewed. This happens by living as communal people, as gathering people, as worshiping people.

Through our prayers, through our singing, through our reflecting on the Word, through our responding and serving, through our participating in the sacraments, through our expressing of hospitality and fellowship, through our interceding in prayer and liturgy for the world, we bring our outside lives into the sanctuary, and we carry the spirit of the sanctuary into our outside lives. We bring our gifts to the altar *together*, where, *together*, they become a communal sacrifice, a communal offering, far greater than the sum of its individual parts because all of its individual members are serving one another even as we serve God.

The preacher, too, is but one of these individual members. Our primary function is as a facilitator of the community's collective, sacrificial work, so our preaching is about more than a sermon. It is about proclaiming the Word through a sermon that functions within a gathering of worship, through which the Word is not merely heard but also embodied in liturgy and ritual for the sake of our communal, spiritual transformation. When the sermon is understood in this way—as one part of a larger whole of worship—it is a proclamation that facilitates Good News in community by connecting the dots between the words of scripture, the words of liturgy, and the words of human experience.

In my own preaching, the introduction to my sermon is often a kind of narration or summary of key moments in worship that we've just experienced together. How did the Call to Worship, or the Confession and Assurance, or the Song of Praise help prepare us for what we're about to hear in the Word? How might this particular moment in the liturgical year help us to experience the Spirit's movement among us in a particular way?

Similarly, the sermon's conclusion is often an opportunity to practice responding to the Good News in a particular way right now, or to point to how we will do so as an act of worship right here, together. Is there a particular way that we need to pray together? Do we need to actually get up out of the pews and engage in some kind of ritual together? If Communion or Baptism are part of the service, how do these sacramental acts help us to live according to the Word just proclaimed?

In order to preach the gospel of justice, we must also live it—as individual disciples ourselves and as members of one body in Christ. We approach the pulpit with sober judgment, according to the measure of faith that God has assigned, praying that the words of our mouths and the meditations of every heart will be holy and acceptable to God (Psalm 19), facilitating the renewal of our minds that is made possible through the living sacrifice of our communal, spiritual worship.

Worship Helps Us Live a Covenant of Justice

Worship is the place where a community gathers to recall, sustain, and reenter the redemptive story in which God has called us to participate. This is where our worldview is shaped by God's heart for the world, by God's heart of *hesed*, by God's heart for justice. We receive and respond to this grace of God, and we practice together how we might live in joy and gratitude and freedom.

God's covenant with us is exceedingly benevolent, and it is also exceedingly demanding. It demands that we see others as God sees us. That we love others as God loves us. That we share in the pain of others as God shares in our pain. The benevolent part of this covenantal equation, however, ensures that these demands are not actually obligations. They are the natural response to minds that have been renewed and transformed according to the mind of Christ. The fruit of our living sacrifice of worship, then, will be doing justice, loving mercy, and walking humbly with God.

Scripture is the story of our faith, the story of our ancestors' human experience as they walked in the grace of God, the story of God's grace for us, and the story of God's justice at work in our world today, even as all of creation groans for the ultimate justice of a New Creation (Romans 8). In order to preach the gospel of justice, we must proclaim Good News that is firmly rooted in scripture's story—the full arc of scripture's story, which is not only the individual forgiveness of sins and promise of salvation, but also the call to participate in the cosmic reordering of power underway even now. We rehearse our role in this story through our practices of worship.

I've suggested that adopting a focus statement like a Core Affirmation for sermon preparation helps ensure that the sermon will declare *both* what God has done for us *and* what we are to offer in response. Our call to action is never primary. It is always in response to God's instigation. Our response is always an outpouring of gratitude in light of the Good News we receive. We respond by seeking justice because we are already recipients of God's justice. This rhythm of receive-then-respond is the rhythm we rehearse in worship.

We give praise to God because we've already received the love of God. A Prayer of Adoration is saying, "We adore you, God, because of all that you've already done to adore us and to love us and to forgive us and to give us more than we could ever ask or even imagine." We confess our sins by turning inward to consider, "What is preventing me from receiving Good News of forgiveness and freedom in Christ?" and are assured that, despite the many ways that darkness surrounds us, we are always walking in the light of Christ. We present our gifts of time, treasure, and talent as an offering to God, the giver of all good gifts.

In every service of worship, we look at God, look at us, and look at God. Sermons that do the same help us to see the justice God is calling us to do, which is made possible because Christ is walking with us in our world, and the Holy Spirit is moving in our midst. It may be tempting to come to worship simply to find peace and serenity, but we must come to worship prepared to do our work—the work of God's people, called to be neighbor-loving agents of a New Kingdom of justice. Liturgy is, after all, "the work of the people."

Worship Helps Us Live a Prophetic Witness

If the preacher is to be a prophetic witness, then worship is the primary venue for testifying. It may be tempting for a preacher to assume the role of jury—examining the evidence of scriptural and social exegesis in order to a render a verdict; or the role of attorney—arguing one position against another; or even the role of judge—attempting to arbitrate the human condition as if holding divine authority. None of these are appropriate postures for preaching because the pulpit is not a place of adjudication but of illumination. The preacher is called solely to testify in prophetic witness to God's grace. Doing so in the context of worship enables that testimony to fulfill its purpose of pointing beyond itself in an act of prophetic imagination.

Worship disrupts the usual patterns of our lives, or at least it offers the potential of disruption. In today's social climate where deep fractures have risen to the surface, driving extreme polarization and destabilization, with fear and anger on the rise, it is perhaps understandable that many of us come to worship seeking a place of refuge, a chance to escape the chaotic currents of change. Certainly, worship does provide some manner of refuge and comfort—that's the Good News part, after all—but worship as escapism is what has enabled the church's numbness. Worship as disruption is an opportunity to not simply ride out the storm of the world's ever-more dangerous currents, but to actually change the way they move.

When we worship along Creator's Good Road, rather than sequestered in a dark sanctuary, we seek wisdom and understanding from "the other." We become curiously open to the presence of truth in the stories, prayers, songs, images, and rituals of people and communities that may be very different from our own. This may be just the disruption we need to begin thinking more creatively about our use of symbols and metaphors, so we can illustrate a much broader and comprehensive story of our faith. We might learn to adjust our narcissistic tendencies and begin to encounter the *imago Dei* in the people and places we have tragically overlooked.

The prophetic witness of the preacher is one grown out of this kind of curious and creative engagement with God. We become adept at encountering revelation in places we might prefer not to visit, and we develop the courage to proclaim this disruptive inbreaking of God's truth. Our prophetic witness, then, makes us askers of questions, stirrers of imagination, facilitators of conversation, students of the marginalized, challengers of the contented, and comforters of the afflicted.

Sunday after Sunday, our repeated liturgical celebration of Christ's resurrection makes plain that our faith, and the symbols of our faith, are continually being made new. They are continually disrupting what we think we know about God's promises and invitations to us. Each time a community gathers for worship; each time scripture is read; each time stories of lament, protest, joy, or celebration are offered at the throne of God; we recognize our human brokenness and rejoice that this is not the end of our story.

The gospel of justice assures us that God's grace has gone before us, calling us to walk a Good Road of Good News. We are not promised an easy journey. We are only promised that walking on this road will renew our minds and help us to discern the will of God. If we allow this to be a prophetic disruption in our lives, we will surely come to see that it is good, acceptable, and perfect.

SERMON—True Worship—Isaiah 58:1–12

Rev. Dr. Mark Labberton
(former President, Fuller Theological Seminary)
Fuller Seminary Chapel | March 2, 2022
Available via Podcast or on YouTube[1]

> Shout out; do not hold back!
> Lift up your voice like a trumpet!
> Announce to my people their rebellion,
> to the house of Jacob their sins.
> Yet day after day they seek me and delight
> to know my ways, as if they were a nation
> that practiced righteousness and did not
> forsake the ordinance of their God;
> they ask of me righteous judgments;
> they want God on their side.

"Why do we fast, but you do not see?
Why humble ourselves, but you do not notice?"
Look, you serve your own interest on your
fast day and oppress all your workers.
You fast only to quarrel and to fight
and to strike with a wicked fist.
Such fasting as you do today will not
make your voice heard on high.
Is such the fast that I choose, a day to humble oneself?
Is it to bow down the head like a bulrush
and to lie in sackcloth and ashes?
Will you call this a fast, a day acceptable to the Lord?

Is not this the fast that I choose to
loose the bonds of injustice,
to undo the straps of the yoke, to let the
oppressed go free, and to break every yoke?
Is it not to share your bread with the hungry
and bring the homeless poor into your house;
when you see the naked, to cover them and
not to hide yourself from your own kin?

Then your light shall break forth like the dawn,
and your healing shall spring up quickly;
your vindicator shall go before you;
the glory of the Lord shall be your rear guard.
Then you shall call, and the Lord will answer;
you shall cry for help, and he will say, "Here I am."
If you remove the yoke from among you,
the pointing of the finger, the speaking of evil,

if you offer your food to the hungry and
satisfy the needs of the afflicted,
then your light shall rise in the darkness
and your gloom be like the noonday.
The Lord will guide you continually and satisfy
your needs in parched places and make your bones
strong, and you shall be like a watered garden,
like a spring of water whose waters never fail.
Your ancient ruins shall be rebuilt;
you shall raise up the foundations of many generations;
you shall be called the repairer of the
breach, the restorer of streets to live in.
—Isaiah 58:1–12

"Today is a time for introspection, self-examination, and repentance," announced Dean of Chapel Brad Strawn as he welcomed worshipers to this interactive Zoom chapel service on Ash Wednesday. "Many believers gather together to receive a mark of ashes on their head or hand, and these words are said: 'From dust you were made, and to dust you shall return.'"

Receiving the mark of ashes is a moment to consider the significance of our earthly lives, where the arc of life continually bends toward death from the very moment of birth. Every living thing will one day wither and die. That is, if sin gets the final word.

Mercifully, we know that sin does not have the final word, which is precisely why each Sunday of the church calendar is a Resurrection celebration. But during the season of Lent, and on Ash Wednesday in particular, we pause to acknowledge the fragility of this finite life, the fact that without the love and grace of God we would be mere dust. Ash Wednesday is the most somber day of worship in the church year, but it is not an unhappy one, and it is certainly not without its own Good News. Ash Wednesday is an opportunity to take a searching, brutally honest look at ourselves, our communities, our world, and consider how we might more fully rejoice in our good fortune as Easter people by more fully offering our whole selves, in our precious finite bodies, as living sacrifices. It is a day to consider to what extent we are engaging in the renewal of our minds through lives of spiritual worship.

Separated by cyberspace in this chapel service, we would not have opportunity to physically feel the mark of ashes on our heads or hands, but in this brief time together, we would remember the circumstances of our mortality, turning to God in a communal practice of fasting, repentance, and prayer. These acts of worship were also woven into our experience of the sermon, as Rev. Dr. Mark Labberton led us in reflection upon the prophecy of Isaiah 58.

This text is an indictment of what Israel took the greatest pride in—its worship. They were, after all, the people called by God by name. It was to them that God had given all of the vision of what faithful worship would look like, and they claimed to be practicing it vigorously, faithfully. Yet, the very point of their greatest pride here becomes the evidence of God's greatest sense of their abandoning him and the purpose that God has set out.

Israel abandoned God. Their worship did not represent a living sacrifice; it was merely perfunctory. *There's a dissonance, a profound dissonance, which betrays that Israel wants the forms of worship, but not the life of worship. They don't want to truly*

109

give themselves. They don't want to look honestly at who they are. They don't want their minds to be renewed. They want to go through the motions of worship, but not the investment in transformative lives of worship. They want God to come when they call, but they are not heeding God's call.

> *Worship is not just what we do in the liturgical context. It's what we do in our living, in our citizenship, in our neighborliness, in our employment practices, in our treatment of one another. Those are the places that show whether or not we are faithful and true worshipers, or whether we are simply trying to pull one over on God. And God says, "I'm just not interested in your 'as if' worship. I'm not duped. I see it plainly—that you're trying to hold me accountable, whereas I'm the one who comes now in these words to judge you."*

This "as if" worship is not particularly unique to Israel. It is a continuing failure on the part of all humanity, all God's people, to take seriously this vital part of God's covenantal communion with us. Isaiah is calling Israel to the kind of living sacrifice of worship to which Paul was calling the early church in Rome, and to which Mark is calling us today. Are we willing to offer every corner of our lives as an act of worship, or do we compartmentalize, offering an hour or two a week to God before getting on with the rest of our lives, *as if* we are people who practice righteousness?

> *We need to ask ourselves every time we are together in corporate worship, "O God, where am I guilty—like Israel, like the Church—of practicing 'as if' worship?" The failure to do that suggests that the God of Israel's name is tarnished*

by our failure to practice. And God thinks that our failure reflects on the character of God in a way that completely undermines the witness that Israel is to have to each other, and to the surrounding nations. Friends, God takes our worship far more seriously than we could ever imagine.

Mark ensures this point is not left to our imagination by pausing here, and in several additional places throughout the sermon, to allow us to practice a corporate act of worshipful self-examination and repentance. The gathered body was invited to consider the ways in which we may be guilty of "as if" worship, where there may be dissonance between what we practice when leading worship or preaching and when we live our lives, where God may be calling us to repentance or change in our approach to worship.

These are the kinds of things that can help us clarify, right at the beginning of Lent, where we ourselves already see the dissonance. And then I want to invite us to think about what it would mean to remember these things throughout this season of Lent, and to let it be a recurrent refrain. "Where, O God, do I need to repent of 'as if' worship?"

In this meditative space, worshipers answered these searching questions in Zoom's chat feature, by which each member's self-reflection, according to their measure of faith, became a corporate act of confession and lament. This public and communal prayer, emanating from private and personal reflection, was a brief moment to practice allowing the renewal of minds that may have grown numb to the purposes of God. *Lord, in your mercy, hear our prayer.*

As Isaiah's prophecy continues, we learn that the fast God desires is one to loose the bonds of injustice. *Friends, is this the kind of fast that we practice? Is this the kind of fast that we're even interested in? Is it a fast that we've somehow distanced ourselves from, believing that, no, really, it's all about grace? It's always and only about grace?* Our worship must not succumb to the utterly false assumption that what God cares about most is our individual, personal failings, requiring us to perform penitential fasts to somehow pay for our sinfulness—which, by the way, is entirely contrary to the gift of grace in the first place. No, the fast that God requires is about being a communal, living sacrifice through which we *integrate the character of God into a life of worship.*

Mark's guiding principle in the relationship between worship and justice is that worship is the reordering of power. He has written extensively about this, especially in his book *The Dangerous Act of Worship: Living God's Call to Justice,* where he argues that the question of "How do we get our worship right?" is not about what kind of music we sing or what furniture is in the sanctuary, but the extent to which our minds are being transformed according to the will of God and the reordering power of Christ. As we become more and more integrated into the character of God, we become more and more attuned to the injustices wrought by disordered power.

What God is saying here to Israel is that *it's also about reordering the power of your own lives and facing the disorder of power that causes many to suffer.* Reordering the power of our own lives means learning both when to lay down power and when to pick it up. As worship tunes our hearts more and more according to the heart of God, we are awakened to places where our relationship with power has become distorted, whether from the side of privilege or from the side of marginalization. *What sacrifice do you feel called to make? Or what blessing do you want to claim? Knowing that, it will require this call for an integration, that what we say and how we live are to be one thing.* Is it to lay down power so another can grow into theirs? Is it to lean into the power of God and lament the powers that be? Is it to protest, to confess, to serve, to heal, to repent, to rejoice? *O Lord, in your mercy, hear our prayers.*

> *Friends, in this final section of these verses, we're given a portrait, a vision of hope. It will require our full engagement, even our sacrifice. A reordering of power in our own lives, a willingness to acknowledge where we have power and where we can lay it down for the sake of others. It also connects, again, what felt disconnected in the opening verses. God's intimacy and presence and advocacy and gracious, even lavish, provision. Springs in the desert. Repairer of the breach.*

There is so much Good News being proclaimed here. Is the call to sacrificial lives of worship a challenging one? Yes. Are we frequently failing to answer that call? Yes. Do we need to continually hold ourselves accountable to more fully answer that call? Yes. But none of this is an obligation from a demanding, tyrant God who is never satisfied. No, our benevolent God of *hesed* lavishly provides for us. As we drink from God's springs of mercy and are healed by God's faithful repairs, we orient our lives in worship as a joyful response of gratitude and genuine desire to participate in God's hopeful vision of justice.

> *It's not about selfish worship. It's not about worship being used as a tool for our benefit. It's about worship that*

reorders power in our lives, so that in fact we show and name God's glory by living lives coherently reflecting God's character, God's actions, God's sacrifice—ultimately made on our behalf, in this very season of Lent, by Jesus Christ, who came to do the kind of fast that this text describes. To become the kind of repairer of the breach. The one who offers water in a desert land. Who calls us to newness of life, to great hope . . . to become people who more and more reflect in word, in liturgy, and in life, the kind of God that we claim to worship. A God of righteousness and justice for the welfare of God's people, and for the welfare of all.

Worship cannot be the place we come solely to have our own needs met. It is not a place of refuge and seclusion. It is the place where we do the hard work of allowing our minds to be renewed according to the character of God and our lives to be sacrificial offerings according to the model of Christ. Worship is where we not only hear about the gospel of justice, but we practice living it. Worship is where we live Good News in community.

Mark is a renowned preacher, author, and theologian, sought after for his pastoral wisdom, his visionary leadership, and his prophetic witness. This simple, reflective meditation may not seem like an adequate showcase of his talent as a communicator, but that is precisely the point. A sermon is never meant to be a showcase of anything other than the Word of God, and while the preacher's creativity, humor, and charisma are gifts that aid in effective gospel proclamation, God is always the star of the show.

In this Ash Wednesday sermon, Mark is simply and humbly guiding listeners through Isaiah's testimony as an act of meditative self-reflection. This is a kind of fast in itself. He is, in a sense, demonstrating worship's ability to reorder power by actually putting the work of the sermon into the hands of the people. He has facilitated a conversation. He has used his sober judgment and particular measure of faith to lead this small corner of the Body of Christ in worship that allows us to practice being members of one another.

Preaching is a tremendous privilege. It is a privilege to be given a pulpit, a microphone, the attention of a gathered body, the trust of listeners that the words of our mouths, not to mention the testimony of our lives, will proclaim the Word of God. This means that preaching is also a burden of power, and we must learn to steward that power wisely. We do so through lives of worship. Not just the worship that we facilitate week after week, but the worship of our own hearts, where we continually ask ourselves: What is the sacrifice God is calling me to make? What is the blessing of Good News God is calling me to proclaim?

The answers to these questions are not mere bullet points in a sermon outline. They are the foundation of a life of discipleship according to the gospel of justice. It is only through commitment to a life of worship that we can fully answer a call to community, participate in a covenant of justice, and embody a prophetic witness.

APPENDIX A

Sermons

Chapter One: "Embodied Community"—Acts 2:37–47

Inés Velásquez-McBryde
(former Fuller Seminary Chaplain;
Pastor of The Church We Hope for in Pasadena, CA)
Fuller Seminary Chapel, October 7, 2020
Available via Podcast or on YouTube[1]

Buenos días church. . .

Esta mañana quiero invitarles a la mesa de mi abuela y como ella encarnó los valores de la nueva familia en los vv.44–47. La nueva familia aquí suena y huele como la sopa de frijoles de mi abuela.

This morning I'd like to invite you to my abuela's mesa (my grandmother's table) and how she embodied the principles of this *nueva familia* in vv. 44–47. The new community here, which I will refer to as "nueva familia" sounds and smells like my abuela's Nicaraguan black bean soup.

Muchos de uds saben que el proceso de cocinar una sopa de frijoles en los viejos tiempos toma 2 días. Mi abuelita me ponía a trabajar y yo tenía que vaciar los frijoles sobre la mesa, y limpiarlos quitandoles las piedras. Dios guarde alguien mordia y se quebraba un diente con una piedra!

The entire process of making black bean soup took two days if you're old school. It was my job to throw all the beans on the table and hand-pick the rocks out of the mix. God forbid you bit into one of those rocks while you were eating! It's the worst sound in the world!

Luego tenia que lavar los frijoles y dejarlos en remojo toda la noche. La siguiente mañana habia que hervirlos mas o menos 3 horas, fijandome que no se secara la porra y añadir mas agua de vez en cuando.

Then you had to wash the beans and let them soak in water overnight. The next morning you would boil them over a period of three hours, and had to constantly watch and add water as needed so they wouldn't dry up.

Solo entonces estaban los frijoles listos para cocinar, añadirle sazon y sabor. La sopa de frijoles de mi abuela era una obra de amor, tomaba tiempo, esfuerzo, especies y a fuego lento.

Then, and only then, were the beans ready to make a soup with all the flavors and spices. My abuela's black bean soup was a labor of love. It took time and effort and spices and a slow-burning fire.

De la misma manera la nueva familia no aparecio de la noche a la mañana. La nueva familia era una respuesta a corazones rotos por la obra de Jesus en la cruz y el movimento del Espiritu entre ellas y ellos. El. v.37 dice que sus "corazones fueron cortados" y preguntaron "¿Que hacemos?"

The *nueva familia* in these verses didn't happen overnight. This *nueva familia* is a response of the hearts broken by the work of Jesus on the cross and the movement of the Spirit among them. Verse 37 says that they were "cut to the heart" and asked that provocative question "What should we do?"

3, 120 personas respondieron a esa pregunta con arrepentimiento. El arrepentimiento comunitario precede a esta familia reconstituida, bautizada por el Espiritu en un amor santo y en una nueva realidad. ¿Seria que ellas y ellos se habian dado cuenta que no solo habian pecado en contra de Dios sino que el pecado no les habia permitido amarse unos a otros?

Three thousand, one hundred twenty people responded to that question in repentance. Communal repentance preceded this reconstituted *familia* baptized by the Spirit in the living love in this new reality. Could it be that they realized not only how they had sinned against God but also how sin had kept them from each other?

Esta historia fue contada por el Espiritu donde el Espiritu es el que crea la historia y las personas son protagonistas en la historia. Tenemos a un Dios que cruza fronteras y rompe barreras, atrayendo a la mesa a personas que antes no hubiesen comido juntos.

This was a Spirit-spoken story where the Spirit is the Story-Maker and the people are the Story-Tellers. This is a Border-Crossing God and a Boundary-Breaking Spirit bringing together to the mesa those who otherwise would not have eaten black bean soup together before.

Pedro se refiere al profeta Joel y como hijas e hijos han recibido la promesa del Espiritu. Cocinar la sopa de frijoles y compartirla con los demas era tambien parte de la historia profetica.

Peter has just quoted the prophet Joel and how daughters and sons would have the Spirit poured over them. And it involved pouring black bean soup and sharing your soup as part of this prophetic story, so nobody would have need.

Otra leccion de la mesa de mia buela era: Echale mas agua a la sopa. Nunca sabiamos quien iba a venir a la mesa, con frecuencia llegaban invitados/as inesperadas. En nuestra conciencia nicaraguense, nadie se quedaba con hambre a la hora de comer, aun si no habia suficiente comida, simplemente mi abuela añadia mas agua a la sopa hasta multiplicarla.

Another leadership lesson from my Abuela's Mesa is "Echale mas agua a la sopa." It said, "Add more water to the soup." You never knew who was going to show up at our table, but often more guests arrived than we were expecting. In our Nicaraguan consciousness, we have that way of life where you don't turn guests away at the dinner hour, even if there's not enough food, so you "add more water to the soup," quietly to make it multiply.

Mi abuela decia: Donde comen 2 comen 3. Un milabro moderno de peces y panes vivian en la mesa de mi abuela. Su mesa era generosa, llena, fiel, gozosa, llena de sacrificio de su tiempo, presencia y recursos, ya sea en tiempos de abundancia o escasez. La comida era un idioma de amor y una señal y maravilla del Espiritu.

My abuela would quietly say, "Donde comen 2 comen 3": where two people eat, three people can eat. It was a modern miracle at her mesa, like the fish and the loaves that lived in my abuela's mesa. My abuela's mesa was generous, filling, full, joyful, sacrificial sharing of her time and presence and resources, however abundant or scarce. Food was a love language and food was a sign and a wonder of God's Spirit, just like in these verses.

Cuando leo este texto con periodico en mano, lo que veo es otra realidad actual. Me pregunto como la mesa de mi abuela y la teologia de familia puede nutrir nuestra Mesa Dividida:

When I look at this text with the newspaper on the other hand, what I see is another contrast community that is more descriptive of our current reality. And it is the job of faith leaders to describe reality. I wonder how my Abuela's Mesa and familia theology could speak into our Divided Mesas. If I were to rewrite verses 44–47 again:

"Todos los que creian estaban divididos y estaban uno en contra del otro. Ya no tenian nada en comun, no compartian el papel higienico durante la pandemia global, no compartian sus recursos con los necesitados; la mayoria de los miles que habian muerto estaban entre las comunidades afroamericanas y latinas. Si alguien buscaba asilo en la frontera, les ponian gases

lacrimogenos, los metian en centros de detención, separaban a las madres de sus hijas e hijos, separaban las matrices tambien de los cuerpos de las mujeres. Dia a dia pasaban menos tiempo compartiendo sus historias, con corazones cinicos y enojados, comian solos en la mesa sin nadie con quien compartir su sopa."

If I were to rewrite verses 44–47, and with newspaper in hand, it would say this: "All who believed were divided and demonizing the other. They had nothing in common anymore, hoarded toilet paper during a global pandemic and hoarded resources that could help the other; the thousands who were overcome by the virus showed how inequity was distributed among black and brown communities. If anyone had need and sought asylum at the border, they would be tear gassed, turned away, or placed in detention centers; children were dismembered from their mother's arms and the women that were left had their wombs pulled out. Day by day they spent less time listening to their life stories together; with angry and cynical hearts, they ate alone with no one else at their table with whom to share their soup."

Los pasos fieles de mi abuela eran simples, alimentar cuerpos y alimentar almas, porque si nuestros cuerpos estan alimentados, tambien lo estaran nuestras almas. De esta misma manera ella y otras mujeres nicaraguenses dirigen la casa y la familia de Dios en la iglesia.

My abuela's faithful steps were to feed bodies and to feed souls, because when our bodies are well, it is well with our soul. In the same way this is how she and other Nicaraguan women led and managed the household of God.

A menudo las mujeres alimentaban nuestras almas como maestras de biblia aun si no se les permitia predicar la biblia desde el pulpito. Las mujeres nicaraguense a menudo alimentaban nuestros cuerpos y almas despues de terremotos, huracanes, guerras. Compartir la sopa de mi abuela es uno de los sermones mas preciosos que mi abuela predico.

Often the Nicaraguan women fed our souls by being Bible teachers even if the context didn't allow them to be pulpit preachers. Often Nicaraguan women in our church fed our community, soul food and real food, after earthquakes, hurricanes, and during the war. Sharing your soup was the best sermon my abuela ever preached and taught me.

Para mi, esta teologia de familia era una señal y maravilla, y testimonio de la presencia viva de Jesus entre nuestra comunidad. Una familia autentica que encarna los valores del Reino, del Dios que cruza fronteras y rompe barreras por el poder de Su espiritu. Este es el poder de la cruz que vemos en Efesios, que Jesus vino a abolir las enemistades y derribar la pared de separacion entre nosotras y nosotros, de ambos grupos creando una nueva familia.

This was a sign and wonder and a witness of the living presence of Jesus in our midst to me. An authentic community that embodied the ethics of this border crossing God and a boundary-breaking Spirit—the same Spirit that resurrected from the dead. That embodied the power of the Cross in Ephesians where Jesus came to abolish in the flesh the enmity, and put to death the hostility, and out of two groups, created one new *familia*.

Mi oracion es que la mesa de mi abuela pueda iluminar, informar y formar las diferentes mesas teologicas y sociales. Que la promesa de Dios pueda fluir por medio del pueblo de Dios y sus mesas generosas. Esta es una obra del Espiritu, donde el aroma de la sopa de frijoles es la presencia del aroma de Cristo.

My prayer is that my abuelita's mesa, and her theology of *familia*, would illuminate, inform, and form our different theological and social mesas and tables. That the promises of God would flow through the people of God and through the mesas that we set. This is a work of the Spirit to sit at Spirit-filled mesas where the black bean soup is the aroma of Christ.

Que nos esta invitando el amor de Dios a hacer ahi donde tu estas? Que nos pide el Espiritu que hagamos? Adonde nos esta llevando el espiritu? Cual es mi siguiente paso fiel para cultivar este tipo de comunidad familiar?

May you ask yourself: What does love look like here? What is the Spirit inviting us to do, there in your mesas? Where is the Spirit taking me and into whose lives? What is my next faithful step to cultivate this *nueva familia*?

Amen and amen.

Chapter Two: "Sacred Allyship"—Exodus 2:5–10

Brenda Bertrand
(Fuller Seminary Chaplain)
Fuller Seminary Chapel, February 2, 2022
Available via Podcast or on YouTube[2]

Before Moses delivered the people of Israel, there were midwives—Shiphrah and Puah—who delivered him and other baby boys, even against the Pharaoh's edict.

Before Moses could cross the Red Sea, there was Jochebed, who built him an ark and, against all odds, saved the life of God's prophet.

Before Moses ever stood before Pharaoh and said, "Let my people go," Miriam stood before Pharaoh's daughter, brokering a transracial adoption deal.

And while Pharaoh enforces a nationwide mandated genocide on enslaved babies, his daughter is collaborating with an enslaved woman to save the very boy who would one day liberate all enslaved people from under her daddy's rule.

Shiphrah, Puah, Jochebed, Miriam, the princess. Let's be honest. Without these women, there may be no Moses. And with these women, Pharaoh's power is thwarted at every turn. These women are baaad.

Pharaoh truly prophesied his own demise when he said, "Kill the boys, but let the girls live," because the women in this text take him up on his offer, and they come alive in bold, courageous, creative, and prophetic ways.

This is one of those few biblical texts where every "hero" in the story is in fact, a heroine. Although God's name is not mentioned, the Spirit lives large in the subtext. Every woman in this story is guided, transformed, and convicted to do justice. She claims her truth versus conforming to the lies she's offered. Each one creatively uses her voice, her power, her privilege, *and her pain* to break the chains of oppression. Because when the girls live, everyone lives.

Let me hear you say it, "When the girls live, everyone lives!"

So these women, even in the midst of the trouble that no one could see and understand, will model sacred allyship amid an oppressive and murderous system. A system where a whole people group is enslaved unjustly. Where a whole generation of baby boys are deemed illegal. The women will step out along the long journey to upend the injustice that they're seeing right in their own backyards. These women will be our lesson guides today. In particular, the Princess.

So, let's go to them, in the beautiful land of Egypt, along the banks of the Nile. I want you to push away those tall papyrus reeds and cattails. I want you to imagine the morning sun is bright and it glints off bloody water. We are about to witness a phenomenon: the privileged and the marginalized: connecting, collaborating, and co-leading. So let's jump in.

In verse five, the princess is on her way to bathe. Can you see her strolling in her morning splendor? She is wealthy, child-free, possibly unmarried. She may take the throne if/when her father and brothers die—or by some other way, as history suggests. She is privileged, and the system protects her. And for this, she doesn't need a guilt trip or a power trip; she needs allyship. She probably needs friendship, but she needs an opportunity to learn and unlearn how to connect with her own humanity and the humanity of others.

There's an enslaved girl on the scene as well. Can you see her? She's crouching in the reeds, and she's been sent by her mother with a life-altering mission. Hide. Watch your brother. Get home safe, and report. If you're seen, don't speak a word. Serve. Play small. Feel the room. Know your place. Know your language. Learn their language. Be your parents' translator. Understand the rules—code switch when you need to. And please, get home safe. Just like the princess, Miriam knows her place.

Friends, it is hard being seen as a problem, to operate in a system built against you. But Miriam doesn't need saving; she doesn't need pity. She needs an ally, an advocate.

These two girls are down by the reeds for different reasons, from different sides of the river so to speak; one has inherited power, the other has inherited powerlessness. And so, privilege and poverty meet. And we need to remember, privilege is a delusion with its own bondage. And marginalization is bondage, and it is oppression. These women are different, but they're both unfree. It is radical to see us all as suffering and unfree, even in our varying degrees of power*less*ness and power*ful*ness. Did you see how we were so moved when we could all see the word cloud? That we're all suffering, and that somehow our individual and collective liberation is possible when we connect to each other's humanity and each other's suffering. Our freedom truly is bound together.

In verses five and six, we're going to see a couple lessons of sacred allyship from these women. We're going to learn from this North African princess how to be a sacred ally. Something that each and every one of us on this call, and on YouTube and Facebook, that we deserve to receive and that we are worthy to give.

In verse five and six, the princess notices something in the reeds and is drawn to it. Say, "Notice."

It's really simple. To be a sacred ally, we must pay attention. We are conditioned to hide what hurts and cover up what requires our courage. But there may be something seeking your attention. We could let it fade away in the reeds, or we could go to it and see, "What is this?" Where is there unfreedom that wants to get untangled and liberated but it must first be noticed? We can't change what we won't acknowledge.

If we get still enough, like we did this morning, if we're ungrounded long enough, like in a pandemic under stay-at-home orders, we may sense where something is off in our lives and what needs tending to. Friends, start looking where you bathe. In your heart, in your home, in staff and faculty meetings, in the classroom, at church, in our neighborhoods, at family dinner. What unfreedom lies awake there that seeks our attention? The princess is present enough to notice what's in her own backyard because allies, sacred allies, they notice.

One theologian said that Jochebed plants the baby strategically to be seen by the right person but hidden from the wrong one. Allies see.

In verse 6, she uncovers the lid, and it's just as she suspects—it's a baby. A crying baby. And the scripture says the princess, "feels sorry." This is more profound than pity. Pity leads to what in DEI work they call, "Performative Action." You know that, and you've experienced it. It's pretty yucky. Where someone feels obligated to act.

But *Indwell* author Hattie J. Lee says, "Pity creates separation, but compassion that comes from empathy helps us to 'suffer with.' It connects us to our shared experience of living in an imperfect world by acknowledging our shared human condition." Friends, we radically belong to each other, in both our belovedness and in our sorrow. Both in our belovedness and in our suffering. I've been asking God, "God, help my heart to break open for the other. To come alive as I become intimate with someone else's suffering, because we are all suffering together." And what an ally notices, and when they are connected with another's suffering, they can then act in a way that empowers versus action that comes from pity, which only perpetuates power dynamics. Action from obligation only perpetuates the power of privilege.

The princess goes from feeling bad *for* him, to feeling bad *with* him, and she comes alive. She's becoming a sacred ally. She's thinking,

"Is this the world my father has created?" Because if she covers that lid, if she pushes that baby downstream, now she is complicit even more in her father's oppressive regime. She doesn't have to be Hebrew to feel human depravity.

I don't need to be an elder to feel ageism. I don't need to be Black to feel oppression. Allies authentically connect with their own humanity, and they name the humanity of others.

In verse 6, the princess exclaims, "This is a Hebrew boy!" This is more than identifying his culture and gender. The Princess is saying, "God, this is what my nation has come to!?! This is what my family has done, where a mother feels her baby is safer in the reeds in a little ark than in her own home? This is what I have been complicit to? This baby is alive, but there are hundreds who are not. This is a Hebrew boy. He's human just like me. He cries just like me. He has a worried mama at home just like I do. My God, I've got to do something. I need him to survive. I want him to survive."

This princess is coming alive, and this boy will live—why?—because she is. Because when girls live, everyone lives. The princess's liberation is part of the Spirit's larger liberative work that's already happening: in the baby's family and the future exodus of an entire nation will be unleashed in her liberation. Friends, this is sacred allyship. To notice. To draw near to what we notice. To name the truth of what is going on in others' humanity, ugly as it is. Because this heart posture leads her to act. Not from guilt, or fragility, or messiah complex—but from love. John Lewis suggests this kind of love leads us to make a good kind of trouble. Allies stir up a good kind of trouble.

There are two kinds of sacred allyship. I want you to look at Miriam in verse seven, as we come to a fast close. She is listening for authenticity that earns trust. Miriam is listening and discerning, because allyship hinges on trust.

The princess' revelation, "This is a Hebrew boy," is met with Miriam's courageous creativity. Miriam offers to find a nurse and races home when the princess approves. Because Miriam discerns that this ally, North African, gorgeous, Egyptian princess is worthy of trust, even in a system that has proven unworthy. The honest truth is that allyship doesn't always go well. This story could have gone terribly wrong. But Miriam took a risk, and it pays off, literally.

The North African woman buys into Miriam's idea, which means she is ok with seeing herself as part of the story, and not the whole or center of it. A faithful ally knows that solutions come from within communities, from the oppressed themselves. The sacred ally knows that though they can provide resources, they are not the source. They know they are not meant to save anyone, speak for anyone, or to make themselves the hero. The ally isn't giving power away, but acknowledging that power, wisdom, and resources exist before and beyond them. An ally who sees power beyond their own as equally valid has truly been liberated for the work of justice, because they can admit their power is limited.

In verses eight and nine, we see the ally circle widen. Jochebed and the Princess are face to face with a baby between them. Miriam, the negotiator and translator, is brokering the deal. Friends, I could barely keep a dry eye when I envisioned this birth mama reunited with her boy. Just hours prior, she's probably rocking on the floor in a corner of her home, faith-filled and grief-stricken all at once. Unable to eat. Unable to speak. Heart completely broken. Tremoring with her postpartum adrenaline. Her body still recovering from a traumatic birth that she couldn't even prove.

And then a knock comes on the door. My God. A knock comes on the door all because a privileged daughter and a marginalized one decided to come alive together. The princess, these women, they're attentive, they drew near, they told the truth of their own and other people's humanity. This leads them to collaboratively act in ways that liberate them all. Who does this sound like? It sounds like Christ, doesn't it? And his liberative work in the world.

Friends—deep breath—we don't have to save the world, because Christ already did it. But we do want to live like him. What Christ came to do as the most sacred of allies was to take on flesh and become one of us. Becoming human just like us. And because he lives, so can we. Friends, no matter your ethnic background, gender, socioeconomic background, you are worthy of this sacred allyship. To be a receiver and a giver of this holy companioning. Of having someone stand with you and beside you, whether they look like you or not.

The next time we see baby Moses, he is a toddler, speaking his mother's tongue—nurtured between two strong women who resist systems. Who could have imagined this outcome? Who could have made this up? And we cannot know what God wants to do through our risks either.

Because when we live, others live.

When the girls live, everyone lives.

In the name of the Father and Mother, God, and Jesus our friend and companion and ally, and the precious Holy Spirit who stays with us always. Amen.

*[**Acknowledgement from Brenda:** In the spirit of the sermon, I must recognize the women who have directly and indirectly encouraged the creation of this sermon. I wholeheartedly want to acknowledge the mid wives and advocates who have walked alongside me on this journey, braving the uncertain and treacherous paths as we birthed this sermon and brought it forth from the depths of the rivers. Their unwavering support and guidance have played a pivotal role in shaping the narrative. They include:*

- *My dear friend Alyssa Miller, who faithfully stood by my side, offering words of motivation such as "Push!" and, with joyous relief, exclaiming, "You did it. She's alive!"*
- *Anna Carter Florence, whose example has taught me to trust my interactions with the remarkable women in the text. She doesn't know me, per se, but her words were big in my ears as I wrote the sermon.*

• *This sermon emerged months after the passing of my precious mother. In truth, she continues to be a profound source of inspiration for all my sermons. She remains a constant source of encouragement, supporting me from beyond as I make space for her voice and the voices of both named and unnamed women in the Bible.]*

Chapter Three: "Through the Unknown"—Mark 4:26-29

Cindy S. Lee
(Spiritual Director;
Doctoral Projects Administrator and Affiliate Professor of Doctor
of Ministry at Fuller Seminary)
Fuller Seminary Chapel, January 25, 2023
Available via Podcast or on YouTube[3]

Confucius asked, "What does heaven say? There are four seasons going round and there are a hundred things coming into being. What does heaven say?"

Lao Tzu said, "When your work is complete, retire. This is the way of heaven."

Chuang Tzu taught, "Being in heaven's care, we are called children of heaven. This is something which cannot be acquired by learning, nor attained by effort, nor understood by understanding. To know how to rest in the unknowable is the summit of knowledge."

In our passage today, Jesus joins a long line of wisdom teachers who talked about a way of life that he called the kingdom of God or the kingdom of heaven.

Jesus also joins a long line of wisdom teachers who taught through parables. In this same chapter, Mark wrote that Jesus did not teach without using parables. What wisdom teachers know is that we can't change people through debate and truth claims, but that stories can somehow form us. In the wisdom tradition, sages don't give answers. They hold the mysteries, they ask good questions, and they tell stories. They give us the space to encounter divine mystery on our own.

In our parable today, Jesus once again invites us into a way of life. To be honest, this was a parable I had never noticed before in my decades of reading the gospels. I wondered if there is something here that I need to pay attention to. What made my brain skip this story all these years? Perhaps this is a parable that often goes unnoticed because it invites us into a way of life that is unfamiliar to our modern ways of life. In this story, the farmer's life is dependent on a process that he doesn't fully know or understand how it works. He is completely dependent on the grace and mercy of the earth to provide year after year. The farmer's reality is actually our reality too, it's just that we fiercely resist this reality. We are so fiercely independent that we resist the vulnerability of this dependence. We resist by trying to know everything and to grow things ourselves.

This parable gently invites us into another way, a more restful way. The story opens our sacred awareness to the mysteries of the earth and the mysteries of God, and you don't have to know everything, and it's okay to depend on others.

You see, historically, we have all been reading the gospels and especially the kingdom parables with colonizers' eyes, thinking that the kingdom is something we make happen, through building, through conquest, through winning and controlling others. Colonizing is both atrocious acts of injustice and violence towards Indigenous communities, and it is a worldview. A colonizing worldview believes that our natural world is for our own utility and consumption and can be controlled, the colonizing worldview is one we've all bought into in our consuming culture. We have all bought into this worldview in our consuming ways. This worldview has easily led then to the false belief that land and other peoples could be taken and used for our own utility, consumption, and control.

Howard Thurman wrote, "Human beings cannot long separate themselves from nature without withering as a cut rose in a vase. One of the deceptive aspects of mind is the illusion of being distinct from, and over against but not a part of nature. It is but a single leap thus to regard nature as being so completely other than us that we may exploit it, plunder, rape it with impunity."

Our relationship to the earth then, reveals the conditions of our own hearts. How have you been fiercely gripping to your sense of control? In what ways have we tried to control other people and even God in the same way that we have tried to control the earth? Control and power are our human response to the fears of what we do not know and losing our sense of control.

In the church, knowledge is a form of control. We have equipped pastors and missionaries to go out and be the ones that know and give the answers rather than to be the ones who guide us through the questions, the unknowns, unexpected, and uncertainties of life.

Seventeenth-century poet Sor Juana Ines de la Cruz wrote, "Oh if there were only a seminary where they taught classes in how not to know as they teach classes in knowing."

In all the kingdom parables, the kingdom is not one that comes through building, or conquest or knowledge. Instead, the kingdom is a way of life received as children receive, celebrated like a banquet, valued like finding something we lost, but it is never forced. We are simply invited into and drawn into this kingdom way, the way of heaven already happening, for all creation already lives heaven's way. When we abstract God, we abstract ourselves. If the kingdom is simply to be understood and accepted through truth statements, then we become walking heads. But if the kingdom is experienced, if the kingdom is lived here and now, then we embody the way of Jesus.

At the very center of this parable is a healing phrase: We do not know how, we do not know how, we do not know how, and that's okay. There is in this parable a beautiful and simple cyclical rhythm found in night and day, sleep and wakefulness. It is a rhythm of watching the earth grow, die, and come to life again. In that rhythm, the earth provides for us and heals us.

In this passage, the earth is both indifferent and generous. "All by itself, the story says, the soil produces grain." The most knowledgeable and experienced farmer or gardener can't actually make life happen. They are still utterly dependent on the grace and mercy of the rain and sun to grow anything at all. This parable recognizes what the farmer doesn't know and what the farmer can't do.

We were never in control. The earth has always been teaching us our utter dependence, all while we've been futilely striving for our independence. The invitation to dependence is restful. The gospel is not dependent on you, I think that's pretty good news. We can let the earth heal us. We can let community care for us. There is freedom in that.

This week we enter another cyclical rhythm of the lunar new year. It is a 15-day celebration and so we're still in it, today is the 5th day. Collectively we enter this this cycle with fragile and tender hearts. We hold our griefs, trauma, anger and confusion. But somehow that makes it even more important that we eat together, that we celebrate life together, that we be in community together. It is our act of resistance to the violence.

I remember when I was young feeling jealous of my relatives in Taiwan because they use two calendars that means everyone gets to celebrate two birthdays. You may think that having two calendars would be really confusing. Isn't my one calendar full and busy enough? These two calendars are a constant reminder to us that the rhythm of the western calendar, that dominates our economies and has come to represent around-the-clock production and consumption, is not the only rhythm of life. The lunar calendar gently reminds us that there is always an open invitation to another rhythm of life, one that our ancestors lived.

Those that created the Gregorian or western calendar valued accuracy. They valued the most scientific and precise way of calculating and living time.

Those that uphold the lunar calendar on the other hand—they were not concerned with accuracy or what humans can measure or control through science. Instead, the lunar calendar invites us to look up. See the moon? See how it changes? So do our lives change too. Just like our parable today, the lunar calendar invites us into a cyclical rhythm of life. What's really different about the lunar rhythm is that anyone and everyone can see the moon. We don't need special instruments. It teaches us a spiritual practice to daily observe the cycles of change. The lunar rhythm is followed in the Islamic calendar as well as the Jewish calendar. Even women's bodies follow the cycles of the moon.

When the ancient Chinese philosophers saw this cyclical rhythm of night and day, moon and sun, they realized that this rhythm acknowledges our reality. That we live in the cycles of celebration and mourning, pain and joy, good and evil. So in our posture of prayer we learn to hold these realities together. Even if we can't explain it, we can't reason it, even if it feels we don't have control, we keep on holding our prayers. We keep on waking and sleeping. We keep on eating. We keep on depending on another. We keep on depending on God. We keep on holding it as our prayer.

And then on the 15th day of the new year, when the moon is full, round and bright we will gather again. We will celebrate again. This time even bigger, brighter and louder. We gather not just as families but as a city. We will light lanterns. Lanterns everywhere, colorful, beautiful and bright, to scare away the evil that taunts us. We will light lanterns to light our steps forward even through the unknowns. We will eat round, sweet, and sticky things to remember our unity and our dependence on one another. And then we will pray. We will recognize our dependence, and may God have grace and mercy on us all. Amen.

Conclusion:
"True Worship"—Isaiah 58:1–12

Mark Labberton
(former Fuller Seminary President)
Fuller Seminary Chapel, March 2, 2022
Available via Podcast or on YouTube[4]

Friends, how grateful I am for the chance to worship together with you today, and to take a few moments on Ash Wednesday to meditate on this profound text in Isaiah 58, verses 1–12.

This text is an indictment. It is, in fact, an indictment of what Israel took the greatest pride in—its worship. They were, after all, the people called by God by name. It was to them that God had given all of the vision of what faithful worship would look like, and they claimed to be practicing it vigorously, faithfully. Yet, the very point of their greatest pride here becomes the evidence of God's greatest sense of their abandoning him and the purpose that God has set out.

It is a remarkable text, and it is dripping with divine sarcasm in the opening verses. This sense of incredible dissonance, as though God could be duped by worship. Duped by Israel. Nothing could be farther from the truth.

In each of the three sections, I will read the text again, I'll create an opportunity for some reflection, and then eventually I'll give you a chance to be able to not only prompt reflections in the chat, but also to share together at the end of each section. I will say, "Lord, in your mercy," and then we will unmute and say together, "Hear our prayer."

The first section, then, of Isaiah 58:1–5.

In this section, God speaks this word of judgment, of harsh, sarcastic, dripping judgment. Israel believes that, somehow, they're pulling one over on God, and God is going to make it clear just how untrue that is. Hear again these verses:

Shout out; do not hold back! Lift up your voice like a trumpet! Announce to my people their rebellion, to the house of Jacob their sins. Yet day after day they seek me and delight to know my ways, as if they were a nation that practiced righteousness and did not forsake the ordinance of their God; they ask of me righteous judgments; they want God on their side. "Why do we fast, but you do not see? Why humble ourselves, but you do not notice?" Look, you serve your own interest on your fast day and oppress all your workers. You fast only to quarrel and to fight and to strike with a wicked fist. Such fasting as you do today will not make your voice heard on high. Is such the fast that I choose, a day to humble oneself? Is it to bow down the head like a bulrush and to lie in sackcloth and ashes? Will you call this a fast, a day acceptable to the Lord?

There's a dissonance, a profound dissonance, which betrays that Israel wants the forms of worship, but not the life of worship. They want to claim that it's God who fails to hear, and God wants to say to them, "No, it's you who failed to hear and to practice faithful worship."

Worship is not just what we do in the liturgical context. It's what we do in our living, in our citizenship, in our neighborliness, in our employment practices, in our treatment of one another. Those are the places that show whether or not we are faithful and true worshipers, or whether we are simply trying to pull one over on God. And God says, "I'm just not interested in your 'as if' worship. I'm not duped. I see it plainly—that you're trying to hold me accountable, whereas I'm the one who comes now in these words to judge you."

Friends, this opening refrain in the beginning of this chapter is an indictment that's familiar to Israel, at least it should be. It certainly has been given in many other forms, but now here again it's expressed at a time when Israel might take its greatest pride in its temple, in its sacrificial system, in all of its rights and rituals and prayers and faithful words. But disconnected from faithful living, it's worship that is bankrupt.

We need, I think, to always allow ourselves to sit under this word. We need to ask ourselves every time we are together in corporate worship, "O God, where am I guilty—like Israel, like the Church—of practicing 'as if' worship?" Rather than true worship that reflects, liturgically, what we believe and affirm and celebrate and seek, and goes out to actually live what we have then claimed for ourselves and about God.

The failure to do that suggests that the God of Israel's name is tarnished by our failure to practice. And God thinks that our failure reflects on the character of God in a way that then completely undermines the witness that Israel is to have to each other, and to the surrounding nations. Friends, God takes our worship far more seriously than we could ever imagine.

When I wrote the book, *The Dangerous Act of Worship: Living God's Call to Justice,*[5] I did so out of a great burden as a pastor. A feeling as though, at that moment, there were all kinds of questions about, "how to get our worship right." They were divisive conversations. They still can be. And yet, here, over and over again in Israel's life, God has called them to this integration of what we profess and of how we live.

So as we begin this season of Lent, I want to invite us to ask ourselves the question, as we hear God's indictment, "In what ways are we guilty of 'as if' worship?"

Let me invite you to use the chat column to respond to that question. In what way are *we* guilty, am *I* guilty, of practicing as if worship, rather than true and faithful worship? Where is the dissonance between what I practice when we're together, when I lead worship, when I preach, and then when I go out and live my life? Where are the dissonances that betray that I am more committed to myself than I am to the God I claim to worship? Where in my worship is God's call to repentance and to lament and to change?

Again, in the chat, take a moment to share some of your reflections. These are the kinds of things that can help us clarify, right at the beginning of Lent, where we ourselves already see the dissonance. And then I want to invite us to think about what it would mean to remember these things throughout this season of Lent, and to let it be a recurrent refrain. "Where, O God, do I need to repent of as if worship?"

Let's take a moment just to be quiet, and then I'll lead us in that brief prayer.

Lord, in your mercy; Hear our prayer.

In the second section of chapter 58, God begins to portray a picture of the kind of faithful worship that he has in mind. Listen to this:

> *Is not this the fast that I choose to loose the bonds of injustice, to undo the straps of the yoke, to let the oppressed go free, and to break every yoke? Is it not to share your bread with the hungry and bring the homeless poor into your house; when you see the naked, to cover them and not to hide yourself from your own kin?*

Friends, is this the kind of fast that we practice? Is this the kind of fast that we're even interested in? Is it a fast that we've somehow distanced ourselves from, believing that, no, really, it's all about grace. It's all about grace, it's always and only about grace? It's not really about life, integrated life that reflects the grace. No, it's just actually God meeting my—or our community's—needs, but failing, utterly failing, to integrate the character of God into a life of worship.

Here it's interesting because, if worship is about the reordering of power, which I think it is, then here what God is saying to Israel is that, indeed, it is about reordering power. And it's about reordering the power of your own lives and facing the disorder of power that causes many to suffer. It's demonstrated in so many dire circumstances—of poverty and disease, of abuse, being dominated by other people. It's in these places that we're called to be new.

So what account would we give? Where is our worship, specifically, unwilling to make the sacrifice? Or, if we are willing to make the sacrifice, to hear the kind of call that God's giving to the sort of fast that he really desires us to claim and to express? What sacrifice do you, perhaps even now, feel called to make in light of this challenging text?

Again, use the chat column to offer your own reflections. To share whatever words might express for you the call of this text to an awakening of your own sense of disconnection from the worship that God desires, and a practiced connection to which we are so strongly called by these verses.

As you continue to place your remarks in the chat, let me just invite us also into a time of quiet.

O Lord, in your mercy; Hear our prayer.

And in this final section, God gives a vision. A vision of what coherent worship would be. A worship that is both honoring of God in the liturgy, and honoring of God in the lives that we live every day—in society, in culture, in communities, in every relationship, in every context, especially where power inequities cause the abuse of others. When, in fact, our power—whatever that is, whatever it might be, however it can be offered up—is meant to be in service of those who are at the margins.

Listen to this vision, and accept it as an invitation to challenge, but also an invitation to great hope. God goes on to say, if you practice this kind of fast:

Then your light shall break forth like the dawn, and your healing shall spring up quickly; your vindicator shall go before you; the glory of the Lord shall be your rear guard. Then you shall call, and the Lord will answer; you shall cry for help, and he will say, "Here I am." If you remove the yoke from among you, the pointing of the finger, the speaking of evil, if you offer your food to the hungry and satisfy the needs of the afflicted, then your light shall rise in the darkness and your gloom be like the noonday.

The Lord will guide you continually and satisfy your needs in parched places and make your bones strong, and you shall be like a watered garden, like a spring of water whose waters never fail. Your ancient ruins shall be rebuilt; you shall raise up the foundations of many generations; you shall be called the repairer of the breach, the restorer of streets to live in.

Friends, in this final section of these verses, we're given a portrait, a vision of hope. It will require our full engagement, even our sacrifice. A reordering of power in our own lives, a willingness to acknowledge where we have power and where we can lay it down for the sake of others.

It also connects, again, what felt disconnected in the opening verses. God's intimacy and presence and advocacy and gracious, even lavish, provision.

Springs in the desert.

Repairer of the breach.

Friends, as you hear this provision in the final verses, I just wonder, what sacrifice do you feel called to make? Or what blessing do you want to claim? Knowing that it will require this call for an integration, that what we say and how we live are to be one thing.

Let's again take a moment to put whatever comments you want in the chat column to this third section of the text. What sacrifice, what promise do you want to name and claim for yourself today and for us as a community and for the Body of Christ?

It's not about selfish worship. It's not about worship being used as a tool for our benefit. It's about worship that reorders power in our lives, so that in fact we show and name God's glory by living lives coherently reflecting God's character, God's actions, God's sacrifice— ultimately made on our behalf, in this very season of Lent, by Jesus Christ, who came to do the kind of fast that this text describes. To become the kind of repairer of the breach. The one who offers water in a desert land. Who calls us to newness of life, to great hope. But it is this process of transformation that Lent prepares the opportunity for, the sacrifice that only Jesus Christ can make, because we will never adequately measure up. But that calls us on in gratitude, to become people who more and more reflect in word, in liturgy, and in life, the kind of God that we claim to worship. A God of righteousness and justice for the welfare of God's people, and for the welfare of all.

> [Praying] O God, in your mercy, may this be so. May we hear, O God, the call to give up worship that's centered on us instead of you. To practice instead a fasting that reflects your character. An ability to make sacrifices because of your own example, and because of the gift that it is of hope that comes from this kind of consistent, enacted worship. Lord, we cry to you in this season of Lent, may we hear your voice. Call us into account. Invite us into a new life, and to offer to us, for the welfare of many around us, a kind of redemonstration of your life, which faithful worshipers are meant to display. Together, we pray, O Lord in your mercy, hear our prayer. Amen.

APPENDIX B

Praxis Resources

Chapter One: Listening to Feedback

When you are listening to verbal feedback—especially when it is immediately following your sermon and your adrenaline is still rather high—try to listen as if you are an impartial third party. Invite your feelings to step aside for a moment, and focus on hearing the precise words the speaker is using. If it's a structured feedback session, take copious notes; if it's an impromptu conversation after worship, repeat key words in your head until you're able to jot them down as soon as possible afterwards. Go back to read over your notes, and listen with fresh ears so heightened emotions or defensiveness don't cause you to miss what may be very enlightening reflection.

When you are reading written feedback, I've found it helpful to absorb it in multiple readings somewhat like Lectio Divina:

1. The first reading is just a cursory look. Don't try to absorb all they have written, just notice what words jump out at you and keep track of the emotions you're feeling. Generally speaking, is the feedback in line with your own reflection, or are you seeing some surprises? Don't analyze yet, just take note of what you're seeing.

   > Pause, pray, breathe, and ask God to show you what you most need to see.

2. Read the feedback a second time and try to hear the sermon again through their ears. Do you remember the point in the sermon they may be referencing in a certain comment? Do you recall what you may have been feeling during that time while you were speaking? What do these comments say to you about what was happening in the room at the time you were speaking? *[This is a great time to watch, or rewatch, the video of your sermon.]*

> Pause, pray, breathe, and give thanks for these listeners God has entrusted to you.

3. Read the feedback a third time and note your emotional responses. Which comments are the most difficult to receive? (These are not necessarily the most critical comments—for some of us the positive reflections are more difficult to receive.) Which comments make you smile? Which make your defenses rise? Linger over those places that cause the strongest reaction in you—whether positive or negative—because these tend to be the places with the most important truths to uncover about yourself. Allow yourself to lean into those feelings until you are able to discern what may be an important new truth. If you're wrestling with a particularly challenging comment, you may need to return to it again later, or perhaps even invite the feedback giver into a subsequent conversation to help you understand more clearly.

> Pause, pray, breathe, and give thanks to God for the gifts you have been given and that were used to proclaim Good News in this sermon.

Chapter Two: Using an Exegetical Journal

An exegetical journal can be a helpful tool to encourage allowing a text to speak for itself, as well as to open up the possibility of personal meditation on scripture above and beyond the pragmatic concerns of preparing a sermon. Below is the template and instructions for use that I provide to students in my preaching classes. In my preaching preparation today, I rarely write a formal journal such as this, but I always work through the same process, doing much of the work in my head and writing only the notes I intend to use in the sermon or that I want to have on file for future recollection.

Sermon Text: Copy/paste your text in the translation you will use in your sermon.

Context: Write two or three sentences about the context to which you will be preaching. Note specifics about your listeners that are important to your preparation of this specific sermon. For example, are you preaching to a group that is primarily of a certain age, gender, or ethnicity? Is there an event in the life of the community that is impacting your listeners right now? Is there a liturgical season or element of worship that should be considered as part of this sermon?

[NOTE: In the following, a "Day" represents one session of study. Sitting down for an hour or so once a day is ideal. If that is not possible, try breaking your sessions into something like an evening, next morning, and later that afternoon, so there are always several hours between sessions.]

Day 1: Set aside your preconceived ideas about the text and try to see it afresh. This is a brainstorming exercise. Lectio Divina is often a very helpful practice at this stage. Try to do this preliminary study session as early as possible . . . maybe several days or even weeks before your actual sermon. This will allow the text to begin percolating in you.

Write some specific bullet point notes indicating:

- Initial observations about the text
- Questions you are asking of the text (You should have lots of questions!)

- Concerns or observations from the world, and especially your listeners' context, that may need to be in dialogue with this text

Day 2: Begin following up on your initial observations and questions. *Resist the urge to turn to commentaries yet!* Allow your own instincts and ideas about the text to develop first, using Bible dictionaries, original language lexicons, and other research aids to help discover answers to questions you raised on Day 1.

- Consider the literary context—How does the genre or form impact your understanding of the text? Its structure? Its boundaries? Do you need to focus on a larger or smaller pericope?
- Consider the historical context—What was happening in the contemporaneous world of the text? What are the socio-political implications of the time?
- Consider the original language—Compare translations or use original language aids to identify key words, especially those that may be understood in a variety of ways.
- Consider parallel texts—What other passages come to mind in relationship to this one? How do they support or challenge one another? How does the full canon of scripture help us understand this particular text better?
- What new observations/connections are you making between text and context?

Day 3 (and more if needed): Continue your own exegetical work. Make connections to your context and contemporary events. A Core Affirmation for your sermon may be taking shape at this point.

- Consider the literary context.
- Consider the historical context.

- Consider the original language.
- Consider parallel texts.
- What new observations/connections are you making?

Day 4 (and more if needed): Now that you've done your own exegetical work in the text, begin consulting commentaries and other biblical resources. If you haven't done so already, you might also consult non-biblical resources, such as literature, films, podcasts, etc.

- Note how your reading is resonating with the work you've already done—that is, what have you found to affirm earlier ideas, and/or what new questions are arising?
- Include any direct quotes (with citations) and/or paraphrased understanding from other sources.
- Even if you don't intend to use these direct quotes in your final sermon, list here anything that caught your attention and may be informing the direction your sermon takes.

Concluding Observations: Having done your exegetical work and additional research in commentaries and other reading, summarize your conclusions in a few sentences. These conclusions should clearly flow from the work you've noted above. Look for ways to synthesize all you have learned, rather than jumping to a new idea you just saw in a commentary, for example.

Core Affirmation Statement: Write a concise description of the central scriptural theme you are proclaiming in the sermon, using the format below (adapted from Brown/Powery's *Ways of the Word*). This theme must address both God's action in the text and what this means for the people's action in response. The Core Affirmation (CA) is written with God's action first because anything a text calls us to do can only be in response to what God has already done. Crafting a precise

CA will help you structure a sermon that naturally proclaims this kind of Good News.

This sermon will declare that because God has/is/ will _____, We are able to/called to/respond by _____.

Bibliography: *A typical working preacher's sermon preparation need not include a formal bibliography, but you may find it helpful to keep a basic list of sources consulted for ease of reference if returning to these notes for a future sermon. I require students to consult a minimum of three sources, at least one of which must be written by a woman or person of color. Most of us could stand to have our go-to sources further diversified.*

Outline: *Every sermon should have a clear Introduction and Conclusion and some level of development in between, listed here as "moves." The shape of your eventual manuscript or outline may grow into something else, but it is often helpful to have these basic moves in mind as a roadmap.*

Sermon Title: (Fewer than 7 words is best)
1. Introduction:
2. Move 1:
3. Move 2:
4. Move 3:
5. Conclusion:

Chapter Three: Spiritual Practices in Creativity

All examples are from *Artful Leadership*, an online, go-at-your-own-pace course available through Fuller Equip at https://fuller.edu/equip/.

Blind Contour Drawing

This practice is not explicitly spiritual in and of itself, but it is a great way to work on learning to see in new ways, and many artists use this as a meditative practice. You will draw the contour of an object in one continuous line *without looking at the paper*. In doing so, your hand is able to record what your eye sees without any interruption from what you *think* you see.

1. Assemble an object you'd like to draw (e.g., a shoe, plant, piece of fruit, animal, face, hand, etc.), a piece of paper, a pencil or pen, and a timer.
2. Tape the paper to your drawing surface so it doesn't move as you draw, and arrange yourself so you can see the object you will be drawing without looking at your paper.
3. Set the timer for 10 minutes (and commit to moving your pencil this entire time).
4. Focus your eyes on some part of the object and begin moving your pencil to record what your eyes observe. Do not look down at the paper as you draw. Rather, force yourself to concentrate on how the shapes, lines, and contours of the object relate to one another.
5. Continue observing and recording until the timer ends.

Do not worry about the quality of your drawing—it is guaranteed to look ridiculous. The goal is to force yourself to practice seeing in a new way and to have the courage to shift your thinking from analytical to more intuitive. Approach your drawing time prayerfully, and you just may find it has more spiritual value than expected.

Singing Prayers

Turn your usual prayer time into singing prayers. No musical accompaniment, just your voice. You can do this in the shower! Feel the reverberations in your body as you create sound with your voice, lifting your prayer in song.

1. Make a short list (either in your head or on paper) of people, situations, joys, or concerns for which you'd like to pray.

2. Choose a word or phrase to sing aloud for each petition. This could simply be a person's name, or a particular request (e.g., *Heal her, Lord* or *Shine your light on them*), or use the same liturgical phrase each time (e.g., *Amen, Lord have mercy,* or *Praise to you, O God*).

3. As you think about each petition, imagine a sound or melody that represents how you feel about the person or situation, and allow this to shape the way you sing the chosen word or phrase. How might your voice convey a prayer of joy as opposed to an expression of grief? You might sing one or two notes like a chant, or sing a whole sentence to a familiar tune (e.g., *Amazing grace, please fall on Jim, And heal his pain and grief. . . .*)

4. Rather than listening critically, try to feel the song in your body as you sing each petition. (You might place the palms of your hands on your cheeks, chest, or abdomen to feel your breath and the reverberations of sound.) Consider whether you are feeling/hearing the sentiment you mean to reflect in your sound. Sing each petition several times until you feel ready to move on to the next. Pause and take a deep breath (or two or three) between each petition. You may wish to end with a final *Amen* or another closing phrase.

Dance Examen

End your day with a traditional "Prayer of Examen" but, in each of the five steps, move your body in a way that describes where you felt God's presence throughout the day.

1. Arrange yourself in a comfortable and attentive posture as you place yourself in God's presence. Give thanks for God's great love for you.
2. Pray for the grace to understand how God is acting in your life as you shift into a posture of openness to God's guiding presence (e.g., palms turned upward; shoulders back and face tilted upward; lying prostrate, etc.).
3. Remain in your posture of openness, breathing slowly and deeply, and review your day—recall specific moments and your feelings at the time.
4. Reflect on what you did, said, or thought in those instances. Were you drawing closer to God or further away? Settle your focus on one particular moment of the day. How does your body respond as you reflect on this moment? Move into a new posture that represents what you are feeling, and remain there for several breaths.
5. Look toward tomorrow—think of how you might collaborate more effectively with God's plan. Move into a final posture that represents your hopes and intentions for tomorrow.

Writing Psalms

Meditate on a psalm of praise (e.g., Psalm 8, 100, 150), lament (e.g., Psalm 6, 10, 130), or testimony/thanksgiving (e.g., Psalm 30, 118); then work on composing your own psalm. Note that psalms are meant to be a communal expression, even as they are written from very personal points of view. You can write a new psalm each day, or add a line or two to the same psalm each day. Here are some things to think about with each type of psalm (adapted from Old Testament professor John Goldingay's classroom exercises):

WRITING A PSALM OF PRAISE:

- Tell us what you will do and/or invite us to join you.
- Declare the reasons why God is praiseworthy—what God always is, key things God has done for us, key gifts from God to us.
- Remember not to be individualistic—this isn't about what God has done to you personally or about what you feel. Think collectively and communally.
- Express yourself in images.
- Reflect on your own experiences but do so indirectly so that other people can identify with them.
- Say things more than once, in different words.

WRITING A PSALM OF LAMENT:

- Decide who are the people in need that you are praying for—your church, your city, your people, some other person in need, or yourself.
- Put yourself in the position of the person or people you are praying for; then pray as them.
- Remind yourself and God of key facts about who God is or things God has done in the past—especially ones relevant to the subject for whom you're praying.
- Tell God about the need—about the facts, the feelings, the fears.
- Tell God you still trust—or can no longer trust—in God's provision, call, presence, and so on.

- Tell God what you want, in one line.
- Listen for God's answer, and/or imagine you have heard God's answer.
- Respond to the answer.

WRITING A PSALM OF TESTIMONY/THANKSGIVING:

- Decide for whom you are testifying (see above lament note).
- Tell us what you are going to do and/or invite us to join you.
- Tell the story of how things were. . .
  - when you were doing fine,
  - how things collapsed,
  - how you prayed,
  - the way God answered, and
  - the difference God's answer made.
- Express how you feel now.
- Say what will be your attitude to God in the future.
- Tell other people what difference this should make to them.
- Talk more about God than about you.

NOTES

Chapter 1

1 Many biblical scholars also believe the letter known as Ephesians was not written by Paul himself, but by someone from the school of Pauline thought at the time. Since it is clearly Pauline theology in either case, I don't consider the question of specific authorship to impact interpretation. If anything, the fact that a "school of thought" was already emerging at the time of the Early Church further affirms the plural, communal nature of Paul's arguments.

2 "Micah Groups," Fuller Brehm Preaching, https://www.fuller.edu/brehm-center/ljo/micah-groups.

3 I am indebted to Micah Group Mobilizers Jin Cho, Joy Johnson, and Bret Widman for this language.

4 "Pastors Share Top Reasons They've Considered Quitting Ministry in the Past Year," *Barna Research* (April 27, 2022), https://www.barna.com/research/pastors-quitting-ministry.

5 Tish Harrison Warren, "Why Pastors Are Burning Out," *The New York Times* (August 28, 2022).

6 This is based solely on my anecdotal observations and not on any formally collected data.

7 Excerpted from Micah Groups curriculum currently in development, with contributions from Jennifer Ackerman, Jin Cho, Joy Johnson, and Bret Widman.

8 Listen to this sermon at https://fullerstudio.fuller.edu/podcast/embodied-community-ines-velasquez-mcbryde. You can also find a

video of the entire worship service for October 7, 2020 in the "Chapel" playlist at youtube.com/fullerseminary.

Chapter 2

1 Jennifer Lynn Ackerman, "Howard Thurman and Sacramental Silence: The Convergence of Worship, Preaching, and Justice," PhD Dissertation (Fuller Theological Seminary, Center for Advanced Theological Study, 2020).

2 Howard Thurman, *The Inward Journey* (New York: Harper and Row, 1961), 112.

3 See Howard Thurman, *Jesus and the Disinherited* (Boston: Beacon, 1949).

4 Otis Moss, Jr., *Backs against the Wall: The Howard Thurman Story*, directed by Martin Doblemeier (American Public Television, 2019), https://www.pbs.org/show/backs-against-wall-howard-thurman-story.

5 Howard Thurman, "Mysticism and Social Change," in *The Papers of Howard Washington Thurman*, Vol. 2, ed. Walter Earl Fluker (Columbia, SC: University of South Carolina Press, 2009–2019), 202–203.

6 I am indebted to Dr. Carolyn L. Gordon for instilling in me this exegetical process. The exegetical journal template that I use today has been adapted from one originally created by Dr. Clayton Schmit.

7 See Thomas G. Long, *The Witness of Preaching* (Louisville, KY: John Knox Press, 2016); Haddon Robinson, *Biblical Preaching: The Development and Delivery of Expository Messages* (Grand Rapids, MI: Baker Academic, 1980, 2001, 2014).

8 Sally A. Brown and Luke A. Powery, *Ways of the Word: Learning to Preach for Your Time and Place* (Minneapolis: Fortress Press, 2016).

9 Brown and Powery, *Ways of the Word*, 142. Emphasis in original.

10 Listen to this sermon at https://fullerstudio.fuller.edu/podcast/sacred-allyship-brenda-bertrand. You can also find a video of the entire worship service for February 2, 2022 in the "Chapel" playlist at youtube.com/fullerseminary.

11 Shane Claiborne, Jonathan Wilson-Hartgrove, and Enuma Okoro, *Common Prayer: A Liturgy for Ordinary Radicals* (Nashville: Zondervan, 2010), 562–563.

Chapter 3

1 *First Nations Version: An Indigenous Translation of the New Testament* (Downers Grove: InterVarsity Press, 2021).
2 Thomas Long, *The Witness of Preaching*, 2nd ed. (Louisville: Westminster John Knox Press, 2005), 99.
3 Walter Brueggemann, *The Prophetic Imagination*, 2nd ed. (Minneapolis: Fortress Press, 2001), 44–45.
4 https://www.fuller.edu/brehm-center.
5 Much of this section is taken from an online curriculum I've written for Fuller Equip called *Artful Leadership*. https://equip-store.fuller.edu/product/artful-leadership.
6 For more on the power of curious questions, see "Courageous Conversations Across a Growing Divide: One Small Step," NPR audio program, October 13, 2020, https://www.npr.org/2020/10/13/912725672/courageous-conversations-across-a-growing-divide-one-small-step.
7 Jennifer Ackerman, *Artful Leadership*, https://equip-store.fuller.edu/product/artful-leadership.
8 Credit for this wonderful illustration of God's faithfulness to us in all of our stumbling belongs to Kelsey Eberth, a former preaching student and prophetic witness in her own right.
9 Listen to this sermon at https://fullerstudio.fuller.edu/podcast/through-the-unknown-cindy-lee. You can also find a video of the entire worship service for January 25, 2023 in the "Chapel" playlist at youtube.com/fullerseminary.

Conclusion

1 Listen to this sermon at https://fullerstudio.fuller.edu/podcast/true-worship-mark-labberton. You can also find a video of the entire

worship service for March 2, 2022 in the "Chapel" playlist at youtube. com/fullerseminary.

Appendix A

1 Listen to this sermon at https://fullerstudio.fuller.edu/podcast/ embodied-community-ines-velasquez-mcbryde. You can also find a video of the entire worship service for October 7, 2020 in the "Chapel" playlist at youtube.com/fullerseminary.
2 Listen to this sermon at https://fullerstudio.fuller.edu/podcast/ sacred-allyship-brenda-bertrand. You can also find a video of the entire worship service for February 2, 2022 in the "Chapel" playlist at youtube.com/fullerseminary.
3 Listen to this sermon at https://fullerstudio.fuller.edu/podcast/ through-the-unknown-cindy-lee. You can also find a video of the entire worship service for January 25, 2023 in the "Chapel" playlist at youtube.com/fullerseminary.
4 Listen to this sermon at https://fullerstudio.fuller.edu/podcast/true-worship-mark-labberton. You can also find a video of the entire worship service for March 2, 2022 in the "Chapel" playlist at youtube. com/fullerseminary.
5 Mark Labberton, *The Dangerous Act of Worship: Living God's Call to Justice* (Downers Grove: IVP Press, 2007).

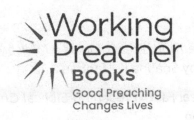

Working Preacher BOOKS

Good Preaching
Changes Lives

Working Preacher Books is a partnership between Luther
Seminary, WorkingPreacher.org, and Fortress Press.

Books in the Series

The Peoples' Sermon: Preaching as a Ministry of the Whole Congregation by Shauna K. Hannan

Real People, Real Faith: Preaching Biblical Characters by Cindy Halvorson

The Visual Preacher: Proclaiming an Embodied Word by Steve Thomason

Divine Laughter: Preaching and the Serious Business of Humor by Karl N. Jacobson and Rolf A. Jacobson

For Every Matter under Heaven: Preaching on Special Occasions by Beverly Zink-Sawyer and Donna Giver-Johnston

Preaching the Gospel of Justice: Good News in Community by Jennifer L. Ackerman

Digital Homiletics: The Theology and Practice of Online Preaching by Sunggu A. Yang